Hearing God's Voice Above the Noise

HEARING
GOD'S
VOICE
ABOVE THE NOISE

STUART BRISCOE

While intended for the reader's personal enjoyment and instruction, this book is also for group study. A leader's guide with Reproducible Response Sheets is available from your local bookstore or from the publisher.

VICTOR BOOKS

A DIVISION OF SCRIPTURE PRESS PUBLICATIONS INC.
USA CANADA ENGLAND

Other Victor Books by Stuart Briscoe

Pulling Together When You're Pulled Apart
David: A Heart for God
What Works When Life Doesn't
Dry Bones

All Scripture references are from the *Holy Bible, New International Version*, © 1973, 1978, 1984, International Bible Society. Used by permission of Zondervan Bible Publishers.

ISBN: 0-89693-002-5

2   3   4   5   6   7   8   9   10   Printing/Year   95   94   93

To Jill,
who because she takes God seriously has taken
her marriage, her motherhood, and her ministry
seriously, and I'm glad.

Contents

Introduction

THE LAST TWELVE BOOKS of our English Old Testament, commonly called the Minor Prophets, were bound together as one volume in the Hebrew Old Testament. They are not called "minor" because they are of minor significance, but because of their brevity. We should never regard them as of minor importance, for what they have to say is of profound significance.

I firmly believe that there is much for us to learn as we study the prophetic statements of Scripture. But first, let me clarify what I mean by prophecy. Usually we think of prophecy as prediction. The primary objective of the prophet in the Old Testament, however, was not prediction. The prophets certainly had a predictive aspect to their ministries, but foretelling was not their primary objective. Thus, when we study prophecy we should not be treating it as a crystal ball through which we can see into the future. We should be looking into the prophets primarily as statements made by men of God who heard what God had to say and relayed that message to their contemporaries. If we proceed in this fashion we will not become so enraptured with peering into the future as in discovering what God was saying to people through men of God. He was desperately anxious that his people should hear his voice, and just one of the things God had to say through the prophets was related to the future. Much of what he had to say was not related to their future at all; it had to do with their here and now.

Accordingly, the prophets were men called by God to hear what God had to say and to stand up and proclaim it to their contemporaries. God had chosen a people for himself, remember, and he had determined that a certain area of the earth would be their land. God was particularly concerned about his people and the land in which they would live. Jerusalem, the capital city of that land, and the temple centered there, were the apple of his eye. Thus over and over again, when God speaks to his people through the prophets, he talks about the land, about Jerusalem and Zion, and about the temple. This temple had profound significance because it spoke of God's dealings with his people and their response to God himself.

As we look into what the prophets have to say, we discover how God's people were failing dramatically to be the people they were called to be. Yet how gracious God was to them as he continued to remind them of their blessings as his people, particularly in terms of the land, the city, and the temple.

These are the themes we are going to be exploring in this book. I make no apology for the tack I will take as we study these striking and significant books of the Bible together, for these prophetic statements have spoken deeply to my heart. I hope they will have as profound an impact upon you as they have had on me.

D. Stuart Briscoe
Milwaukee, Wisconsin

*Hearing
God's Voice
Above the
Noise*

One

THE FAITHFULNESS OF GOD
Hosea

WE CAN DETERMINE fairly accurately when Hosea prophesied because he gives us the names of a number of the kings of Judah who were reigning while he was writing. As a prophet to the northern kingdom of Israel he tells us that Jeroboam II was the monarch at the time. And it is clear from the list of contemporary rulers in Judah, the southern kingdom, that Hosea was also ministering during the reigns of others who followed Jeroboam.

This was a particularly horrendous time in the history of Israel. In 2 Kings 15 we find the story of Jeroboam II and his successors. One, for instance, reigned six months and then was assassinated. His assassin then reigned for one month and he in turn was killed. And things just went from bad to worse. Anarchy was abroad. In this kind of environment Hosea was called to prophesy.

Hosea was a very unusual man, and he is a classic example

of a prophet who doesn't just talk, but who lives his message. Hosea's message was a shocking one, and his life was equally horrifying.

A Marriage of Obedience

First of all, we need to note the significance of his marriage to Gomer. Hosea 1:2 says that the Lord told the prophet to take to himself this particular woman. Thus his marriage was a clear-cut matter of obedience.

You will notice, however, that this woman Gomer, whom God told him to marry, is described as an adulterous wife who will produce children of unfaithfulness. God says that Hosea is to marry this particular woman as an object lesson to the people of Israel. This unlikely marriage will model the condition or the relationship between Jehovah and Israel.

There are two main ways to interpret this marriage. Many say this is an allegorical situation and that God is simply telling Hosea to engage in a relationship that will symbolize the condition of Israel before she submits to Jehovah. Those who argue for this point of view, of course, point out that the children's names all have allegorical significance. However, the problem with that interpretation is that if Hosea is just acting out an allegory, how could it have any impact on the people to whom he was going to speak? These people weren't dealing in allegories; they were involved in real life. I find it difficult to think of Hosea simply as allegorical.

I know of no allegorical significance in the name Gomer, and nowhere in this passage of Scripture are we given any indication that Hosea should be read as an allegory.

The other way to interpret Hosea is to accept this as a literal situation, that Hosea really did marry Gomer and that she was as the Bible describes her, "an adulterous wife" who produced "children of unfaithfulness." If we take this interpretation we must ask ourselves what was going on. Some people would say that Gomer was formerly a temple prostitute, that she had engaged in licentious living, and that she had now come out of this life—but her history was well known. They say Hosea married her and subsequently she returned to her old life. Others say, no, she was not like this, but God knew from the beginning what would happen. She was pure when Hosea married her, but she was going to turn bad. A third possibility is that she was actively involved in prostitution, and that God told Hosea to marry a practicing prostitute.

We can discuss and debate these matters but it is impossible to come up with any conclusive answer. It is best to face the facts: that Hosea found himself married to Gomer, that she was unfaithful to him, and that she bore children who were not his children. It is altogether possible that the first child, Jezreel, was Hosea's child, but it is highly unlikely that the other two were. Scholars are divided in their opinion on this. One thing is very clear, however. Hosea is married to an unfaithful wife who bears children who are not his. Then she goes off and deserts him. In all of this she models what Israel had done to Jehovah.

There is a second significant aspect to Hosea's experience: his children and their names. His first child was a son named Jezreel. Then Gomer gave birth to a daughter named Lo-Ruhamah. The third child was a son named Lo-Ammi. Each of these names has an inherent, profound significance, a deeper meaning that was a part of the message Hosea was commissioned to preach to Israel. Some commentators have pointed out that these three children were born over a period of about ten years. The sad events recounted took place over a long, extended period. What an unhappy marriage Hosea and Gomer were modeling before their children and the community in which they lived! Their situation simply reinforced the message Hosea was preaching. Even the children's names were a part of that message.

What's in a Name?

"Then the Lord said to Hosea, 'Call him Jezreel, because I will soon punish the house of Jehu for the massacre at

Jezreel, and I will put an end to the kingdom of Israel. In that day I will break Israel's bow in the Valley of Jezreel' '' (Hosea 1:4, 5).

Jezreel was to be a powerful object lesson. The very name, Jezreel, would take the people back in their minds to the time of a particularly obnoxious king and queen, Ahab and Jezebel. Though they had plenty of property of their own, they coveted the vineyard of Naboth, a Jezreelite farmer. This man's vineyard, which had been handed down from generation to generation, unfortunately adjoined Ahab's palace at Jezreel, and the king wanted it badly. His evil wife Jezebel plotted how to get the land from Naboth. By hiring false witnesses to testify against the farmer, she got the land for Ahab and had Naboth stoned to death. For her evil actions, Jezebel came under the judgment of God and later died a horrible death at the hands of Jehu. In his own time, Jehu came under God's judgment and he, too, died and was buried in Samaria. Jeroboam II came from the stock of Jezreel, Jezebel, and Jehu, and he, too, lived a life that was utterly repugnant to God. For that reason the name Jezreel, given in Israel at the time of Hosea, would be a constant reminder of a time in Israel's history that was abhorrent to God. God is so angry with Israel that he is going to "put an end to the kingdom." Hosea's son is a reminder of Jezreel's sad, bloody history, a reminder that God has said final judgment will come upon Israel in the valley of Jezreel, when the nation of Israel will be broken and put to an end.

Then Gomer gives birth to a little girl, Lo-Ruhamah. This name means "not loved," or "not pitied." What a name for a little girl! What pressure Hosea must be living under, with a wife like Gomer, and a daughter who is, in all probability, not his child at all! Through her birth God is saying to Israel: " 'Call her Lo-Ruhamah, for I will no longer show love to the house of Israel, that I should at all forgive them. Yet I will show love to the house of Judah; and I will save them—not by bow, sword or battle, or by horses and horsemen, but by the Lord their God' '' (Hosea 1:6, 7).

The little boy, Jezreel, had been among them; the prophecies had come to them. But still they hardened their hearts, refusing to listen. So God sends this little girl to impress his message upon them. God says, "I will not pity my people Israel, but I will relentlessly bring the judgment that I have been warning them about for a long time." Notice the thrust of Jehovah's message to his people. On the one hand he says, "I will not pity Israel, the northern kingdom, but I will pity Judah. I want Israel to be an illustration to Judah of what can happen if they do not arrange their lives according to my orders." So now we have two children in this sad family as mobile object lessons.

Still the people continued in their sins, and so a third child is born, a second son. And his name is Lo-Ammi. Lo-Ammi means literally "not my people." The people of Israel, of course, were proud of the fact that God had called them out of Egypt. They boasted of how he had preserved them in the wilderness, driving out their enemies before them in Canaan. They entered the Promised Land he had given them and were proud of the covenant that God had made with their father Abraham. Often they talked about the fact that he would be their God and they would be his people. But now God, through little Lo-Ammi, makes a dramatic, startling statement. He is born into a world of terrible circumstances, so through him God tells Israel, "You are no longer my people." How overwhelming this must have been to this proud people! Jehovah is saying, "I have totally rejected you."

We are used to hearing people reject God. But the sovereign Lord reserves the right to reject those who reject him. I have met people who feel they can actually reject God with impunity. "It doesn't matter," they say. "It will all work out in the end." What they seem to overlook is this fact: The sovereign Lord is perfectly free to deal as he chooses with those who reject him. And the sovereign Lord is saying through this third child of this sad family, "You people who pride yourselves in being my people—you people who abuse the privileges of being my people, who claim to be my people but live like the devil, you'd better hear something and you'd better hear it real good. You are no longer my people!"

Theologians have argued for centuries over what Hosea is really saying. Some say God had made an unconditional covenant with them and it didn't matter what they did; Israel would still be his people. These interpreters are really saying, "They are God's people as far as their standing is concerned, but they will not experience the blessings of being the people of God."

Other scholars would say it means what it says. These people were given the privilege of being the people of God; God reached out to them sovereignly and drew them to himself, but they failed in their responsibility and reneged on their commitment to God and the covenant. Therefore the covenant was annulled—they are no longer God's own people!

We can have a marvelous time discussing this. I believe what the Bible says. God is a God of justice as well as a God of love. In this case, Israel had blown it. They had turned their backs on God too many times! Those who were once loved are no longer going to be pitied and those who call themselves the people of God at that day will no longer be God's people.

A Marriage Gone Bad

The third thing that happens is recounted in chapter 3. We are not given any of the sordid details. The adulterous Gomer has deserted Hosea and after she deserts him, she engages in all kinds of adultery. Ultimately she reaches the point of utter destitution. Notice the personal tone that emerges in Hosea 3: "The Lord said to me, 'Go, show your love to your wife again, though she is loved by another and is an adulteress. Love her as the Lord loves the Israelites, though they turn to other gods and love the sacred raisin-cakes.' So I bought her for fifteen shekels of silver and about a homer and a lethek of barley. Then I told her, 'You are to live with (wait for)* me many days; you must not be a prostitute or be intimate with any man, and I will live with (wait for) you' " (vv. 1–3). The prophet immediately goes on to explain the significance of what he is saying: "For the Israelites will live many days without king or prince, without sacrifice or sacred stones, without ephod or idol. Afterward the Israelites will return and seek the Lord their God and David their king. They will come trembling to the Lord and to his blessings in the last days" (vv. 4, 5).

There is a powerful message in this marriage gone bad. Gomer's unfaithfulness, her desertion of her husband, her liaison with another lover, her slide into prostitution, her other lover's abandonment of her, and her descent to a place of complete humiliation, are not detailed for us. How do we know it all then? Because Hosea goes and buys back his own wife from whomever had bought her. And the price he pays for her—fifteen shekels—is significant. Remember how much the traitor Judas received for the Lord Jesus? It was thirty pieces of silver. Thirty pieces of silver was the price of a slave. Fifteen shekels was the value of a slave at half-price—the price reflected that this slave was "damaged goods." That's how low Gomer had fallen! Hosea's experience portrays what was actually happening as far as the relationship between God and his people was concerned.

A Marriage With Meaning

Now we come to the most beautiful part of the story. Against this dreadful backdrop of a ruined marriage, we see a picture of Hosea's loyalty and forgiveness. Despite her terrible sin, the prophet goes to his wife. God has told him to show love to his wife. How unthinkable in human terms.

---

* Words of Scripture in parentheses are alternative readings supplied in the marginal notes to the New International Version.

God still calls Gomer "your wife." Even after what she has done, in spite of how low she has fallen, there is a covenant of marriage to be honored. And Hosea honors his commitment to Gomer. In spite of her sin, he continues to love this woman who has abused his trust and dishonored the marriage bed. When God speaks to him he is willing to forgive Gomer and pay the redemption price to bring her back to himself. Notice that he goes for her at the place of her destitution. In all probability he brings her back home and lovingly cares for her. Their reconciliation allows her to receive strength, nourishment, and healing. She has a chance to think things through and come to repentance, rejecting her old life.

A definite sequence of events follows. Hosea tells her that he will wait with her, and she will wait with him, for many days. During that period her prostitution and her adultery must not reoccur; she will have time to come to her senses, to repent.

Look at the uncompromising nature of Hosea's message. Generally speaking, it is quite clear. First of all, the covenant of marriage that has been established between Hosea and Gomer is a picture of the agreement God has made with his people. God loves to use the analogy of marriage. This is one reason why we believers should be so desperately concerned about the attitude toward marriage in our present day. Marriage is intended to model the covenant that God has with his people. But as marriage covenants become more and more meaningless under the pressures of our age, the model becomes less meaningful.

In Jeremiah 2:2, Jehovah says: " 'I remember the devotion of your youth, how as a bride you loved me and followed me through the desert, through a land not sown.' " The analogy is very beautiful: Jehovah as the bridegroom came down into Egypt and received to himself his bride. He remembers the love of his bride. She even followed him into the wilderness without any visible means of support, living all those reckless, beautiful days of first love. Now, of course, that covenant has been broken by unfaithfulness and adultery. Notice that God insists on speaking in a similar analogy to Israel in Hosea 2. He says, " 'I will betroth you to me forever; I will betroth you in righteousness and justice, in love and compassion. I will betroth you in faithfulness, and you will acknowledge the Lord' " (vv. 19, 20).

A Love Relationship

An important Hebrew word is used here—*hesed*. It is translated many different ways in the Old Testament. Some people say it is related to the idea of the covenant, therefore it has the idea of loyalty. Others say it suggests we become involved in a covenant because we have a prior love that makes us want to enter that covenant, so the idea of *hesed* is steadfast love. Other people say this loyal love demonstrates itself in kindness and generosity and mercy, and in many instances you will find the word *hesed* translated as all these different words. One word used in the older translations probably capsulizes the whole meaning: *loving-kindness*. What God says is this: When he makes a covenant with his people, it is a covenant of loyalty, love, kindness, and tender mercies which he expects to be reciprocated. The sovereign Lord reaches out and says, "I will be your loving, kind, loyal, generous God. Respond to me in love as a bride responds to her husband, and be loyal and loving and generous and kind and open and warm in your relationship to me."

This is the fundamental message of Hosea. Isn't it sad that this covenant Jehovah has made with Israel has been broken through the unfaithfulness of God's people? Read what God says: "Hear the word of the Lord, you Israelites, because the Lord has a charge to bring against you who live in the land: 'There is no faithfulness, no love, no acknowledgment of God in the land. There is only cursing, lying and murder, stealing and adultery; they break all bounds, and bloodshed follows bloodshed" (4:1, 2). He is talking about the people of God. This was what was happening to those covenant people to whom God had been pouring out *hesed*—loyalty, love, kindness, mercy, tenderness, generosity. What had been the reaction? What had been the response of the people of God? They had reciprocated with no faithfulness, no love, and no acknowledgment of God.

This can be illustrated in many ways from Israel's history and from Hosea's prophecy. I want to identify, however, only two basic things here. First, *the unfaithfulness of idolatry* and second, *the unfaithfulness of immorality.* In Hosea 4 Jehovah says, " 'My people are destroyed from lack of knowledge. Because you have rejected knowledge, I also reject you as my priests; because you have ignored the law of your God, I also will ignore your children. The more the priests increased, the more they sinned against me; they exchanged their [my] Glory for something disgraceful,' " (vv. 6, 7).

God's main charge against his people is their lack of knowledge of God. This in turn leads to a lack of *acknowledgment* of God. This means, of course, that their relationship with God is all wrong. That is the fundamental problem, which eventually found them sliding into idolatry.

From the very beginning when the Israelites went into Canaan, God told them to have absolutely nothing to do with the cultic religions of the Canaanites. In Hosea 9:10 Jehovah describes the situation: " 'When I found Israel, it was like finding grapes in the desert; when I saw your fathers, it was like seeing the early fruit on the fig tree. But when they came to Baal Peor, they consecrated themselves to that shameful idol and became as vile as the thing they loved.' " What a picture! "Grapes in the desert . . . early fruit on the fig tree." Then—vileness.

God had revealed himself to his people. When they came into the land of Canaan, they were told to worship Jehovah exclusively. The worship of the Canaanite gods could not exist alongside the worship of Jehovah. But what happened? As soon as they reached Canaan, they began to intermarry with the Canaanites. They began to assimilate Canaanite religion. In no time they began to lust after the idols of the Canaanites. So bad did this idolatry become that Jeroboam I, when he became king of Israel, breaking away from the southern kingdom of Judah, said, " 'It is too much for you to go up to Jerusalem. Here are your gods, O Israel, who brought you up out of Egypt' " (1 Kings 12:28). The "gods" he made were two golden calves, similar to those used in Baal worship. He told the people that they should simply worship the calves he set up in the two strategic cities of Bethel and Dan. Worship became a matter of convenience, a matter of identifying with the culture, a matter of simply doing things their own way rather than God's way. This situation became so bad that the people utterly confused Baal, the god of the Canaanites, with Jehovah, the God of Israel. This is portrayed rather dramatically in Hosea 2:16 " 'In that day,' declares the Lord, 'you will call me "my husband"; you will no longer call me "my master." ' " The translation unfortunately hides an important fact brought out in the Amplified Bible—" '. . . you will call Me Ishi or My Husband, and you shall call Me no more Baali or My Baal.' " So confused had the Israelites become, as they moved into Canaan, they found themselves following Baal. They had assimilated Canaanite thinking; they had neglected to do things Jehovah's way. Now they were so confused that they simply thought of Jehovah as a "super-Baal."

A Subtle Slide

Look what has happened. The Israelites have made God in their own image. One of the most insidious things that can happen to God's people (it has happened over and over, throughout human history) is this. We humans try to remake God in our image. This is the great problem confronting the Christian church in Africa today. The church founded by the missionaries in Africa had much of the white man, much of colonial thinking in it. And the African has begun to reject what he sees as colonialistic. In many instances, however, they have begun to assimilate much of indigenous African religion into the Christian church. Thus we see instances of various kinds of witchcraft going on within the church. It is possible that a total assimilation of that which is anti-God could arise in the church.

Let me cite another illustration. In much of Latin America you will find evidence of the remarkable advance Roman Catholicism has made there. But you frequently discover in the very graphic paintings on the walls of the Roman Catholic churches not only Christian symbolism, but also the symbolism of the various native tribal groups. Symbols that are the exact opposite of all that Christ stands for appear on their walls.

What's Happening on the Home Front?

Let's bring this closer home. There is also a very real possibility that God's people here in North America in the twentieth century are remaking God in our image. We emerge with a God wrapped in stars and stripes. We finish up with a God who endorses everything we endorse to make us comfortable. One of the great dangers we face at the present time is that of producing a national religion that presses Jesus Christ into the mold of being the all-American boy.

Instead of the Christian church becoming that which sits in judgment on American society, the Christian church becomes a cheerleader for American society. Increasingly we are removing ourselves from the reality of God and Christ. Much going on even in American evangelicalism today leaves many of us deeply perturbed, for the Jesus Christ who is being portrayed in many areas of evangelicalism today is not the Jesus Christ who overthrows the temple tables. He is not the One who speaks out against hypocrisy, the One who will have nothing to do with false piety and empty religion. The Jesus Christ who is portrayed in much of American evangelicalism today is a very laissez-faire Christ, a champion of free enterprise. This Jesus sees everything as black and white in terms of Communist or anti-Communist.

We need to be careful at this point, because we may be making the same mistake the Israelites did as they began to worship a God remade in their own image. They ignored the God who had revealed himself from heaven, who transcended all cultures and placed them under his critical eye. This was their sin; this was the unfaithfulness of Israel—the unfaithfulness of idolatry.

The Unfaithfulness of Immorality

To pinpoint the unfaithfulness of immorality for you I am going to draw on Hosea's own marvelous literary skills. He is the master of the simile and the metaphor. In one or two words he can paint a marvelous picture.

" 'The Israelites are stubborn, like a stubborn heifer. How then can the Lord pasture them like lambs in a meadow?' " (4:16). Have you ever tried to get a heifer to go where it doesn't want to go? I remember as a boy on the farm being pushed all around by stubborn heifers who didn't have the slightest intention of doing what I wanted them to do. The immorality of Israel is like this. They point-blank refuse to do what God is telling them to do.

God has told them openly; he has warned them. Hosea and Gomer have lived among them, their children have been born and are growing up among them. Hosea is preaching his heart out. But, like stubborn heifers, the Israelites take no notice. They refuse to change.

Look at what God says! " 'What can I do with you, Ephraim? What can I do with you, Judah? Your love is like the morning mist, like the early dew that disappears' " (6:4). What a picture! Have you ever seen the morning mist? Have you noticed how long it lasts when the sun comes up? When the heat comes on, the mist is gone. Like stubborn heifers, the people of God persist in doing evil no matter what God says to them. Then occasionally they get teary-eyed and repentant. "I'm going to turn from that thing," they say. "Never again will I do it. I am going to love the Lord." You know what happens. Their love is like the morning mist.

Notice how God further describes them—"They are all adulterers, burning like an oven . . ." (7:4). There is another dramatic picture for you. God is not talking now symbolically. He is talking about sexual immorality, about people burning and lusting after each other, hopelessly out of control. They are burning and blazing after each other like hot ovens. So hot, he says, is this oven, " 'the baker need not stir . . . [it].' " What a dramatic picture of the sexual immorality that apparently was going on among God's people.

The Lord goes on describing them in Hosea 7:8— " 'Ephraim mixes with the nations; Ephraim is a flat cake not turned over [or half-baked]." The picture here, of course, is the flat bread or cake that is cooked on the hot coals. In the Middle East, it is still done this way. They get the coals red hot and then they slap the dough into the pan; it sizzles and cooks quickly. Then the baker turns it over and cooks the other side. And it's delicious. But you can get one burned to a cinder on one side and soggy and mushy on the other.

God is saying about Israel that they just don't seem to understand the two sides of being God's people. On the one side they adhere to what he teaches and they even put it into practice in their lives. Strangely enough, the Israelites, while they are engaging in their idolatry, are going through all the external motions of Jehovah worship. But on the other side, there is no application of these things.

Put another way, they are into all the principles of religion, but when it comes to the practicality of it, they are half-baked. They are deeply into the theology of the whole thing, but when it comes to the ethic of it, they are half-baked. When it comes to attending church, they are great—

but when it comes to applying Christ in their daily lives, they are half-baked. A dramatic picture again.

Look at Hosea 7:11: " 'Ephraim is like a dove, easily deceived and senseless—now calling to Egypt, now turning to Assyria.' " Israel is like a silly dove, fluttering after this one, fluttering around after that one. They react to every situation that comes without any sense of direction, without any sense of content or significance.

In verse 16 we find another metaphor: " 'They do not turn to the Most High; they are like a faulty bow.' " Did you ever try to shoot an arrow from a bow? You get everything absolutely right, you pull it back and let it go, and the thing goes right off the side. Why? The bow is twisted. No matter how you pull it, how you aim, if the bow is twisted the arrow is going to go off the side and miss the mark. That describes the people of God in Hosea's day. They are like a faulty bow.

In Hosea 8:9 God says, " 'They have gone up to Assyria like a wild donkey wandering alone. Ephraim has sold herself to lovers.' " Hosea certainly knew how to get his message across, didn't he? Israel is like a wild donkey wandering alone, sniffing after this and sniffing after that.

A final metaphor appears in Hosea 10:7. "Samaria and its king will float away like a twig on the surface of the waters." The events of history are going to catch up with you, the prophet says. The people of God are going to be swept away. This is the sad picture of the unfaithfulness of God's people.

All That Ends Well . . .

The story doesn't end there, however.

I'm so glad that Hosea didn't end at chapter 13, because the following chapter shows that God still loves them despite their sin. In the same way, Hosea relentlessly loved his unfaithful wife, Gomer. Even though he must deal with her firmly and lead her to repentance, still he goes on loving her. In an identical way, Jehovah, the covenant God, will

remain lovingly, loyally faithful to his people even though
he has cut them off in order that they might come to repentance and return to him. The certainty of judgment has
come through loud and clear. God's judgment is unequivo-
cal. But the people's love will be like the morning mist.
Like the early dew it disappears when the sun grows hot.
Like the shafts of straw on a threshing floor, like smoke
escaping through a window—this is the quality of our human love. But God's love endures. Hosea 14 shows what
is in store for God's people because of that love:

> Return, O Israel, to the Lord your God.
> Your sins have been your downfall!
> Take words with you
>   and return to the Lord.
> Say to him: "Forgive all our sins
>   and receive us graciously,
>   that we may offer the fruit of our lips.
> Assyria cannot save us;
>   we will not mount war-horses.
> We will never again say 'Our gods'
>   to what our own hands have made,
>   for in you the fatherless find
>   compassion."
>
> I will heal their waywardness
>   and love them freely,
>   for my anger has turned away from them.
> I will be like the dew to Israel;
>   he will blossom like a lily.
> Like a cedar of Lebanon
>   he will send down his roots;
>   his young shoots will grow.
>
> His splendor will be like an olive tree,
>   his fragrance like a cedar of Lebanon.
> Men will dwell again in his shade.
> He will flourish like the grain.

He will blossom like a vine,
  and his fame will be like the wine
  from Lebanon.
O Ephraim, what more have I to do
  with idols?
  I will answer him and care for him.
I am like a green pine tree;
  your fruitfulness comes from me.

Who is wise? He will realize these things.
Who is discerning? He will understand them.
The ways of the Lord are right;
  the righteous walk in them,
  but the rebellious stumble in them.

Isn't this a marvelous picture of Jehovah-God's long-suffering love? How thankful I am that God doesn't treat me as I deserve. Instead, his overarching love continues on despite my failures and shortcomings. What a picture of God's great grace the prophet Hosea gives us!

T w o
THE DAY OF THE LORD
Joel

LITTLE IS KNOWN about the prophet Joel. He wrote the book that bears his name, and his father's name was Pethuel. That is about all we know for sure. But even though we know little about him and cannot even pinpoint the time in which he lived, his message comes across loud and clear.

The first thing that I want to point out in this brief prophecy is that Joel is addressing a contemporary situation and is investing it with a profound interpretation. That is the key to the first part of Joel. There has been a natural disaster. In the first four verses of the first chapter the prophet speaks about devastating swarms of locusts that have destroyed the vegetation of the land. The locusts named in the Bible are like massive grasshoppers. They came in swarms so thick they would literally block out the light of the sun. Moving across an area like an avenging army, they would totally devour all the vegetation.

In this case, not only had the locusts eaten everything, a dreadful drought had already brought Judah to the brink of starvation.

A Natural and a National Disaster

Joel interprets this not only as a natural disaster, but a national disaster, too. He points out in chapter 1 how almost every aspect of community life had been affected. He cries to those given to wine, "Wake up, you drunkards, and weep! Wail, all you drinkers of wine; wail because of the wine, for it has been snatched from your lips" (1:5).

Then he goes on to point out that it is not just that the drunks cannot get their booze now. The entire economy of the land has been ruined. The domesticated animals are suffering deeply. Even the wild animals have nothing. And "the priests are in mourning" (1:9).

Food and drink are now in short supply. The whole nation has ground to a halt. Joel cries: "The swarms of locusts have come, the drought has come, and we are in desperate circumstances."

Then he takes a quantum leap. In verse 15 he laments: "What a dreadful day!" We have no difficulty understanding why he said that. A natural disaster has precipitated a national disaster. This deserves the expression, "What a dreadful day!" But he goes on: "For the day of the Lord is near; it will come like a destruction from the Almighty."

At this point, Joel begins to interpret the twin disasters and says categorically, "There is a definite link between this natural disaster and divine activity."

"The Day of the Lord Is Near"

As we study the prophets, both major and minor, we come across this expression, "the day of the Lord." It appears frequently in the New Testament as well. It is a fundamental aspect of Hebrew thought, an ongoing concept in Hebrew theology. At this particular moment in Judah's history, however, as Joel observes the dreadful condition of his land, he links it to the day of the Lord and says it is imperative that the people realize what is happening. It is important that they recognize in this national disaster that God is at work, bringing judgment against his people for their sins.

His statement raises questions: Are we to interpret all natural disasters as divine activity? Are we to interpret natural disasters as the activity of Satan? Or are we to interpret some natural disasters as divine activity and some as the malicious activity of Satan permitted by a gracious God to bring judgment upon a rebellious world?

I don't know the answer. This is a very difficult, profound subject. But I do think I know what Joel would say about his contemporary situation, under the inspiration of the Spirit.

First of all, in Joel's mind, there is no question about the link between what is happening to the land and God's displeasure with his people. Joel is calling the people's attention to certain things.

Let's apply this biblical truth to our situation today. We must always be prepared to accept the fact that God is constantly at work in our circumstances. We must always listen to him and prepare to take him seriously. This is true for us as individuals, and it is true for our nation as well. It's true for the other nations of the world, too. God has never left himself without a witness, and he is always at liberty to intervene as he chooses.

Joel says to Israel that the God of justice is moving in the affairs of his people, making it clear that his people have sinned and that he, as the God of justice, must punish them. This particular natural disaster, Joel is pointing out, is either God's punishment for sin, or a reminder of the ultimate disastrous day of judgment—"the day of the Lord," which will come.

Joel goes on to demand that the people of God declare a holy fast. They are to call a solemn assembly, summoning the elders and all who live in the land to the house of the Lord their God to carry out their vows to the Lord. As the spokesman for God, Joel calls for a national time of repentance, a national time of prayer. Calling the people as a nation to repentance, he demands that individuals come before the Lord in prayer for the spiritual needs of those among whom they live. All this is abundantly clear in the opening chapter of Joel.

A Message of Hope

In chapter 2 the prophet sounds the alarm in an intensified form. And at the same time he injects a message of hope. As we look at the nature of God through the eyes of the prophets we discover that God always has a double strand in his message. On the one hand he reminds his people that he is a God of justice, a holy God who will not tolerate sin. On the other hand, he also reveals that he is a God of grace and of mercy, longing and loving to forgive his erring people, on the basis of their repentance. That is why Joel sounds the alarm, but at the same time adds a message of hope and grace. "Blow the trumpet in Zion; sound the alarm on my holy hill. Let all who live in the land tremble, for the day of the Lord is coming," he says (2:1, 2).

Again we see that theme—the day of the Lord. But notice: he is insisting that this serious situation demands a serious response. Some Bible expositors read Joel 2 and say that the prophet is simply reiterating what he has said in the first chapter. The locusts and the swarms are just like invading armies and Joel is restating what he had to say, and intensifying it, either because the people wouldn't listen at first or because another swarm of locusts is coming.

Other interpreters look at the passage and say that Joel is moving now from the swarm of locusts and predicting that enemy armies are going to flood the land just as the locusts did. He is sounding the alarm because there is going to be a mighty invasion.

My personal conclusion is that Joel is not talking about

little armies, but that he is simply intensifying his language to drive home the message. The swarm of locusts, the drought, the natural disasters—they all prefigure that awesome day of the Lord. This requires a serious response, for the situation is serious.

Joel then points out that if the people will come up with a serious response to God, if they will listen to the alarm, if they will come to the solemn assembly, in repentance before God, their serious response will be the very basis of blessing.

" 'Even now,' declares the Lord, 'return to me with all your heart, with fasting and weeping and mourning.' Rend your hearts and not your garments. Return to the Lord your God, for he is gracious and compassionate, slow to anger and abounding in love, and he relents from sending calamity. Who knows but that he may turn and have pity and leave behind a blessing . . ." (2:12–14).

What is Joel saying? If the people will respond to God and recognize that he is intervening in their affairs, if they will return to the Lord, if they will repent of their sin, there will be blessing and not judgment. Notice what he says: They are to rend their "hearts" and not their "garments."

Returning, Not Rending

What God is looking for is not mere external activity. He is interested in heart attitudes that spill over into external activities. Hence Joel says to the people, "Don't come with all the external activities of mourning, tearing your clothes to show how deeply concerned you are about this situation, but still with an unrepentant heart. Don't dare to do that. It is far more important," he says, "that we come before the Lord with a broken heart because of our sin and that of our society."

All manner of external activities and professions are valueless if they do not stem from a heart that is deeply repentant. Our attitudes should flow from a heart desperately

concerned about the spiritual condition of society as a whole
and the people of God in particular.

"Return to your Lord," Joel says.

How easy it is for the people of God to become so involved
in all manner of activities that they forget the Lord whom
they profess to love and serve. Not long ago I talked to a
gentleman involved in full-time ministry. I had shared with
him from Ephesians 1, how God wants to enlighten our
hearts so that we can come to know him better. In effect
his reply was: "I have been so busy in the Lord's work
that I have had no time for the Lord." If that is true of a
person devoting himself to full-time ministry, how easy
could it be for the man or woman with all the demands
of secular society placed upon him or her? How easy it is
for God's people to become so immersed in secular concerns
that they leave the Lord out of his position of Lordship
in their lives.

Joel has a message for us, and it is this: If the Lord has
slipped out of the position of Lordship in your life, return
to him. Is sin encroaching on your life? Is sin rampant among
the people of God? Is sin pervasive in the secular society
of which you are a part? Don't just mouth your concern
about it, but come before the Lord with a deeply contrite,
broken heart. This is the serious response Joel demands,
because of the serious situation that exists.

Joel goes on to say that if the people do this, they will
rediscover the true nature of God. He says, if you return
to the Lord, you will discover again how gracious and compassionate, slow to anger, and abounding in love he really
is. Our views of God become perverted and twisted when
our hearts are far from him. When we look at God through
the prism of our own lack of commitment, our own outright
sinfulness, a warped image results. But when there is a returning to the Lord there is a clarifying vision. We rediscover
the Lord. Notice how Joel says that no one is exempt from
this demand to return to the Lord. Even the children who
are being nursed at the breast must come, and those on

their honeymoons must leave their honeymoon and come to the solemn assembly (v. 16). No matter what their situation, *everyone* must make it an absolute priority to repent, for the judgment of God against sin is about to fall.

Joel has a message for the church of God in America today, and it is this: Everything indicates that the day of the Lord is near. Ultimately God, in justice, must judge sin. Sin is rampant on every hand. And the people of God must make it their top priority to come before the Lord, with broken hearts, repentantly, returning to him and beseeching his blessing.

In this prophecy Joel goes on to point out the blessings that will come as a result of this national repentance. First will come material blessings, and then spiritual rewards as well. God is going to restore to them all that they lost and give them, through the outpouring of the Spirit, blessings that will be so rich that God's people will be a blessing to the ends of the earth.

God does this to preserve his credibility. The enemies of the Lord are always quick to criticize. If they see the people of God suffering from swarms of locusts, drained by the drought, their economy in shambles, they blame God. "These people served God," they will say, "and look what their God has done to them!"

What does God say through the prophet? He says, "I will repay you for the years the locusts have eaten. . . . You will have plenty to eat, until you are full, and you will praise the name of the Lord your God, who has worked wonders for you; never again will my people be shamed" (2:25, 26). God is concerned about material blessings for his people; he preserves his credibility among his secular critics and offers practical solutions for practical problems. But he is also concerned that his people, when they are blessed materially, will attribute their blessing to God and bring all the blessings that they have before him in thanksgiving.

There is an erroneous notion abroad at the present time.

Some preachers and teachers select passages from the Old Testament and use them to prove to their own satisfaction that God wants everybody to be healthy and everybody to be wealthy. They even go so far as to say that if you are not healthy it is because of sin in your life, and if you are not wealthy it is because of lack of faith. We need to be very careful before we accept such a conclusion. When God promises material blessing in the Old Testament it is usually to the people as a whole—to the nation, not to individuals. Furthermore, if God blesses an individual it is in order that such wealth be used in service to others and not squandered on one's self.

But Joel is primarily concerned with spiritual blessing. In his thinking, there is a natural link between spiritual blessing and material welfare. Notice the spiritual blessing he speaks of. After material blessings have come, and after the people have turned in repentance to the Lord, there will be a mighty outpouring of the Spirit of God.

"And afterward,
  I will pour out my Spirit on all people.
Your sons and daughters will prophesy,
  your old men will dream dreams,
  your young men will see visions.
Even on my servants, both men and women,
  I will pour out my Spirit in those days." (2:28, 29)

This, of course, was picked up by Peter in his famous sermon; he saw this as being fulfilled on the Day of Pentecost, when the Holy Spirit was shed forth. The spiritual blessing God is promising to a people who are hardened toward him is this: After he has put things right materially as an evidence of his activity on their behalf, he will pour out his Spirit. The emphasis here is that instead of there being an isolated voice of one prophet, like Joel, there will be a proliferation of prophets. He says "your sons and daughters will prophesy, your old men will dream dreams, your young men will see visions." And not just the men! The women will prophesy too. A vast host of people, filled with the Spirit of God, will be shouting loud and clear what the lone voice of Joel is saying. That's the great day of blessing. And that is something God promises to his people through Joel.

Not only that, but in verse 32 he points out that when this kind of loud proclamation is made, people will call on the Lord. "And everyone who calls on the name of the Lord will be saved; for on Mount Zion and in Jerusalem there will be deliverance . . . among the survivors whom the Lord calls" (v. 32). The Apostle Paul picked up on this in Romans 10 and extended it, saying, "Whosoever, Jew or Gentile, shall call on the name of the Lord, shall be saved."

So, at the same time Joel makes his solemn proclamation, he makes a statement of hope. As God's people return to him with broken hearts and acknowledge him as Lord, he pours out his Spirit. As he pours out his Spirit in their lives, they begin to speak and live the truth of God in a confused society. And as they do that, men and women hear the message, turn to the Lord, call on him, and innumerable companies of people are saved. What a marvelous message of hope that is.

A Great Day Coming

In the third chapter, Joel predicts a future "day of the Lord": " 'In those days and at that time, when I restore the fortunes of Judah and Jerusalem, I will gather all nations and bring them down to the Valley of Jehoshaphat' " (3:1).

Commentators, theologians, students, and scholars disagree about this, but "Jehoshaphat" is not a literal valley. The meaning of "Jehoshaphat" is simply, "the Lord judges." We might even call it "the valley of verdict." Joel is telling us that at the same time God brings untold blessing to the people of God, he is also going to gather the nations into the valley of verdict where he will judge them. "There I will enter into judgment against them" (v. 2).

As we read on, God begins to speak very forcefully of how he will judge the nations in that final day of the Lord. Why? Because they have offended God. Why have they offended God? Specifically, in Joel's time, because of their offenses against God's people which thwarted God's purposes. God will finally judge the nations of the world because they have rejected him.

Notice that his judgment will be absolutely just: "I will swiftly and speedily return on your own heads what you have done" (3:4). There is a relentless justice about the judgment of God. What a man sows, he will also reap. For the unrepentant, those who have thwarted the purposes of God, a great and dreadful day of judgment awaits them. God will bring before him the multitudes who have rejected him and give them exactly what they deserve. His retribution will be unyielding in its justice.

What an awesome, terrible thought Joel captures here: "Multitudes, multitudes in the valley of decision! For the day of the Lord is near in the valley of decision" (3:14).

I don't believe that the prophet means the people are making a decision about God. The valley of Jehoshaphat, the valley of decision, is where God judges the nations. God is making a decision about the multitudes who have rejected him.

Even though Joel is speaking forcefully of that judgment of God, in the same breath he speaks of the grace and the mercy of God. In verse 16 he says, "But the Lord will be a refuge for his people, a stronghold for the people of Israel." God has made a covenant with his people. In effect he says, "I am your God and you are my people. I commit myself at all times to be a refuge for you, a stronghold."

Who knows the form in which the judgment of God is going to come? Nobody knows, but that it will come we *do* know. The covenant people of God will be preserved and protected at that time, we also know. Some say God will take his church out of this world before the great and terrible final judgment comes. Others say we will still be here. Still others say we will be here for part of it. One of these days we will find out who was right!

We do know certain things, however. We know that a final, cataclysmic judgment is coming. The judgment of God will be against those who have rejected him. They will be absolutely, meticulously, and relentlessly judged. Thank God we know this too: God's people (at all times and particularly at that time) will find in the Lord their refuge and stronghold.

Joel has come a long way from the drought and locusts with which he opened his book. He has interpreted this situation and sees in it a statement concerning the great and dreadful day of the Lord. Let me conclude by pointing out some practical lessons.

First, God is God and we had better believe it.

Second, God will triumph finally and cosmically, and nobody will hinder him.

Third, God's judgment is absolutely certain and totally just.

Fourth, God is prepared to deal in grace and mercy with those who are truly repentant.

Fifth, God's people should never abuse the grace of God and fall into the spiritual decline of Joel's day. Joel had to tell them, "Rend your hearts and not your garments. Return to the Lord your God," and discover in him all that you need.

The final practical lesson is this: Read, mark, learn, and inwardly digest the third chapter of Second Peter. There Peter takes up that theme of the day of the Lord and projects it in even sharper focus. I believe it will be a powerful message for us in this day, for Peter sees the day of the Lord as the time when the heavens and earth will dissolve with fervent heat. He asks: If we know what will happen in the day of the Lord, that great judgment day of the Lord, what sort of people ought we to be? And he answers his own question. You will find the answer as you study these words for yourself:

First of all, you must understand that in the last days scoffers will come, scoffing and following their own evil desires. They will say, "Where is this 'coming' he promised? Ever since our fathers died, everything goes on as it has since the beginning of creation." But they deliberately forget that long ago by God's word the heavens existed and the earth was formed out of water and with water. By water also the world of that time was deluged and destroyed. By the same word the present heavens and earth are reserved for fire, being kept for the day of judgment and destruction of ungodly men.

(2 Pet. 3:3–7)

Doesn't this make you think of the day in which we live—and the people among whom we live? Yes, the prophet Joel's message is applicable to our day as well!

Three
HEARING WHAT GOD HAS TO SAY
Amos

AMOS PROPHESIED in the days of Uzziah, king of Judah, and was a contemporary of Isaiah and Hosea, both of whom outlived him by a few years. "Neither a prophet nor a prophet's son," Amos was a dresser of sycamore trees and a herdsman. Amos took aim at the people of God and castigated them for their failure to hear the words of the Lord.

The first verse of his prophecy gives us the setting: "The words of Amos, one of the shepherds of Tekoa—what he saw concerning Israel two years before the earthquake, when Uzziah was king of Judah and Jeroboam son of Jehoash was king of Israel." A passage late in the book provides more detail: "Amaziah the priest of Bethel sent a message to Jeroboam king of Israel: 'Amos is raising a conspiracy against you in the very heart of Israel. The land cannot bear all his words. For this is what Amos is saying: "Jeroboam will die by the sword, and Israel will surely go into exile, away from their native land." '

"Then Amaziah said to Amos, 'Get out, you seer! Go back to the land of Judah. Earn your bread there and do your prophesying there. Don't prophesy anymore at Bethel, because this is the king's sanctuary and the temple of the kingdom.'

"Amos answered Amaziah, 'I was neither a prophet nor a prophet's son, but I was a shepherd, and I also took care of sycamore-fig trees. But the Lord took me from tending the flock and said to me, "Go, prophesy to my people Israel." Now then, hear the word of the Lord. You say, "Do not prophesy against Israel, and stop preaching against the house of Isaac."

" 'Therefore this is what the Lord says: "Your wife will become a prostitute in the city, and your sons and daughters will fall by the sword. Your land will be measured and divided up, and you yourself will die in a pagan country. And Israel will certainly go into exile, away from their native land" ' " (Amos 7:10–17).

Look, too, at Amos 8:11–14.

Amos was a man who heard the Word of the Lord and took it seriously; he showed that he took it seriously by obeying God. Even though what God told him to do was very unusual and terribly difficult, he did it. He went from his native village, Tekoa, in Judah, and traveled all the way to Israel. There he began to tell the people of Israel what God wanted them to know—a message they didn't want to hear!

The tremendous burden of Amos's ministry is this: He is so convinced of what God is saying, so committed to what he commands, that he expects the people to be as convinced and committed as he. But he discovers that is not the case.

Early on, he has this dramatic confrontation with Amaziah, the priest of Bethel. This is the man who as a priest should have been ministering the Word to the people. But Amaziah tells Amos bluntly, "Get out of here. We don't want you around here, and we don't want what you have to say. Go home. And if you want to preach, preach there. But don't do it here in Bethel. On your way, you seer. Earn your money back home."

But Amos doesn't back off. He stays on and ministers, sharing with the people the desperate message of a holy God. Through him, God says something very significant: "People of Israel, you've had a boundless opportunity to hear the Word of God. You've had untold opportunities, but you have relentlessly and consistently ignored the Word of God. You have relentlessly and consistently disobeyed the Word of God. Therefore, God says, 'I am going to send famine among you. Not a famine of bread. Not a famine of water. No, something much worse is coming: a famine of hearing the Word of the Lord.' The time will come when you will no longer be in tune with what God has to say."

Actually, the prophet Amos is speaking to us today as well, telling us how important it is to hear what God has to say. So let's look more closely at what he is saying so we can see how it all fits together—and how it applies to us.

God Has Spoken

Amos is convinced that God has spoken. Read Amos 1:2: "The Lord roars from Zion and thunders from Jerusalem; the pastures of the shepherds dry up, and the top of Carmel withers." He likens God's voice to the sound of a roaring lion. The prophet has a tremendous sense of the majesty of God and the authority of his Word. As far as he is concerned, he has left his normal job to proclaim the majesty of God and the authority of his Word. Amos has become obsessed with listening to God.

God's roaring like a lion does not fit our image of God today. We have various images of God: 1) He is our friend. 2) He is our Father. 3) He is our Creator. 4) He is our Savior. All these are valid concepts. But they should not be our only pictures of God. He is also like a lion roaring, demanding attention.

It is obvious that Amos's ministry never recovers from hearing the roar of the Lord. Over and over he proclaims, "This is what the Lord says" (see verses 3, 6, 9, 11, and 13). This same phrase appears three times in chapter 2 also. Repetition can be an evidence that the preacher is unprepared, or it can demonstrate that he has a point worth emphasizing. When Amos says eight consecutive times in a very carefully structured piece of writing, "This is what the Lord says," he is obviously trying to get a point across. The people need to listen!

When God Speaks

In chapter 3 his words are slightly different: "Hear this word the Lord has spoken against you, O people of Israel. . . ." In chapter 4 his language is graphic: "Hear this word, you cows of Bashan on Mount Samaria. . . ." In chapter 5 he cries, "Hear this word, O house of Israel, this lament I take up concerning you. . . ." Throughout the entire book Amos's message is the same: "This is what the Sovereign Lord showed me . . ." (7:1, 4, 7). "I saw the Lord standing by the altar, and he said . . ." (9:1).

Having heard the Lord from heaven, Amos echoes that roar with his own voice. He is trying to get the people to hear what God the Lord has to say. That is the burden of his prophecy. He reminds me of the TV commercial, "When E. F. Hutton speaks, people listen!" You know the setting. Various activities are going on—people are talking together, or a crowd is going and coming in an airport or a sports stadium. Then someone mentions his stockbroker's name, and everybody freezes. How revolutionary it would be if those of us responsible for ministering the Word of God would hear God roar from heaven, and then, in the hush that followed, we could share that with the world around us. It could reverberate in our own hearts and voices so that we would speak in such a way that people would freeze—and listen. This is exactly what Amos did—and he hoped the people of Israel would stop and listen.

Unfortunately, by and large the people ignored God's voice and message.

When God speaks, do I listen? When God roars from heaven and wants my attention, do I stop talking and listen? Or is my life so busy that I listen only now and then? Do I only listen to God when it doesn't interfere with the normal course of events? Or have I been so arrested by what God says that I stop dead in my tracks to listen?

Amos describes his feelings this way: "The lion has roared—who will not fear? The Sovereign Lord has spoken—who can but prophesy?" (3:8). Amos is sensitive to what God has said to him, and submissive to what God is telling him to do. We have observed these qualities about him in the way he describes his call. Amos was not a professional prophet. He had no intention of going into the ministry, but there he was! He must have been perfectly happy working on his farm, dressing his fig trees, just doing his normal duties.

But then the Lord roars from heaven and says, "Amos, there's something I want you to do." Amos replies, "What is it you want me to do?"

"I want you to become a prophet."

I can almost hear Amos asking, "Who, me? I'm a farmer." And God replies, "I know you're a farmer, but I want you to become a prophet."

"Where do you want me to become a prophet?" Amos asks. "Around here?"

"No," God says, "I want you to leave your home in Judah, and go to Israel. They won't like you, because they have broken away from Judah. I'm sending you to a tough place with a tough message. I need a tough farmer like you to do it, and you're my man."

What happens when a person takes the Word of God seriously? Amos is a good example. He heard the Lord roar from heaven. He listened, and he was submissive, even to the point of leaving his farm to do something he thought he would never do. He was submissive enough to leave the place of comfort and go where he was not comfortable. There he preached to people who didn't want to hear him.

A Response to a Response

Amos is a picture of what happens when people take the Word of God seriously. As we've already pointed out, Israel resented the prophet's word. Amaziah the priest accused Amos of inspiring a conspiracy against the king "in the very heart of Israel." He tells Amos: "The land cannot bear all [your] words" (7:10). Amaziah was not above lying, saying that Amos has foretold that Jeroboam will die by the sword. Actually, Amos did not say that at all. He had announced judgment on the family of Jeroboam.

This is the kind of thing Amos had to suffer as a prophet of God. He was misquoted and unappreciated. There was overwhelming resentment against him and the negative reaction against his message was widespread. The people didn't want to hear it, so they told him to go home.

I know something of what Amos experienced. Not long after I came from England to America, I tried to preach the Word of God and apply it to the American scene. Some people became so upset with me that they angrily demanded that I go home. "If you don't like it here, go back to England," they said. "If you earn more money here than you earned preaching there, tough! Go back and earn your living there; but don't talk to us as you have been talking." I'm still here so, obviously, what they said did not go very deep. I solved my problem quickly. After being here five years, I became an American citizen. Then I said: "What do you mean 'go home'? I *am* home."

It was not as easy for Amos. I can understand how he must have felt. The people reacted to him by resenting what he was prophesying and being unwilling to receive the message he was giving out. Both he and his message were rejected. The Lord had roared from heaven; Amos had heard the roar and done what the roaring Lord told him to do. He had passed on the message faithfully—and the people rejected it. But that is not the end of the story.

" 'The days are coming,' declares the Sovereign Lord, 'when I will send a famine through the land—not a famine of food or a thirst for water, but a famine of hearing the words of the Lord,' " declared Amos (8:11). A divine principle emerges here. God will react to Israel's rejection. God will speak, his servants will echo his words, and the people will either hear or refuse to hear. But that is not the end of the matter. Jehovah has the final word. He will deal with the people's response, and we should never, ever forget that.

Let me bring this closer to home. Many people attend church services consistently. They hear the Word of God regularly. But even though they are present in body, I wonder about their spirits. It is possible to become hardened to what God says, to go on blithely disobeying or ignoring what God says. That is not the end of the matter. Know this: The Sovereign Lord Jehovah will respond in kind to our reaction to his Word. Some who go on relentlessly hardening their hearts to what God is saying need to be alerted to the fact that they cannot do so with impunity. God could send to them a famine of hearing the Word of the Lord.

Notice, I didn't say that he would send a famine of *the Word of God.* If I find myself in a situation where the Word of God is not available to me, that's a famine of that kind. But Amos is saying something different. It is possible to be where the Word of God is being proclaimed, where the Word of God is available, but as far as *hearing* it is concerned, the people may as well not have it anymore. The Bible doesn't register. They have resisted the Word for so long that they no longer hear it. A famine of hearing the Word of God has gripped the soul and it makes no impact at all.

This must be one of the most frightful experiences a person could have, because if he no longer hears God's Word deep in the heart, he has lost touch with reality.

He is no longer in touch with the One who controls the universe.

A simple rule applies here. If you don't *heed* the Word of God, it's only a matter of time before you will no longer *hear* the Word of God. Remember what Jesus told his disciples? If they stayed too long in a certain place, the people would no longer hear them. They were simply to shake the dust off their feet and go to the next town. This is why Jesus sometimes remained silent in the presence of important personages. It happened during his trial before Pilate. On one occasion Jesus told his disciples that they should no longer cast their pearls before swine. The people whom he called "swine" had reached a point of famine in hearing the Word of God. Sometimes people reach the point of famine in hearing the Word of God. This is a very definite result of God's action.

Do I take God seriously? Do I take what he *says* seriously? Do I *heed* what he says? Or do I think I can treat him with benign neglect and it doesn't matter? "Hear the word of the Lord," Amos says. If I don't *heed* it, the time will come when I will no longer *hear* it. When that time comes I will be out of touch with reality.

Eight Burdens

Though he was only a simple farmer, Amos could really preach. And he also knew how to use psychology. He comes quietly into Israel, speaking the Word of God, and they don't want to hear him. They refuse to listen and give him a hard time. But God has eight messages for them.

"How on earth am I going to get these people to listen?" Amos asks. So he tells them, "The Lord has roared from Zion, and this is what he says about Damascus" (author's free translation, see Amos 1:3). The Israelites detested Damascus, so Amos had a crowd in no time at all. Once he has their attention, he tells them all that is wrong with Damascus and outlines what God is going to do with this neighbor to the east.

Next Amos tells them what God would do to the Philistines, particularly Gaza, their neighbor to the southwest (1:6–8). The Israelites hated this enemy, so, by the time Amos is through clobbering the Philistines by sharing his second burden, he has attracted a large crowd. I can almost hear the people wondering who is next on his list of neighbor nations.

Then Amos trots out Tyre, their neighbor to the north (1:9, 10), and Edom, their old enemy to the southeast (1:11, 12). Amos tells his audience what is wrong with Edom and promises the judgment fires of God upon them.

When he is through with Edom, the crowd is even larger, so he starts in on Ammon, his fifth burden—which also lay to the east (1:13–15). He moves on then to Moab (2:1–3), and the crowd's response is absolutely marvelous. The people love it; they are so thrilled to learn that God is going to deal with their sinful neighbors in judgment.

Then Amos gets to Judah, his seventh burden (2:4, 5). The Israelites are so upset with Judah that they are rather pleased to hear what God is going to do with them. By this time Amos has the congregation eating out of his hand. They all recognize that people sin and that God is just. And they all concur that the justice of God demands that sin must be punished.

But then Amos quits preaching and goes to meddling! Burden number eight turns out to be Israel itself! It is doing the same things the other people are doing. With relentless consistency and without apology, Amos simply says, "All you people who are so thrilled to hear that the judgment of God will come upon the sins of the people you detest, hear this. You had better shape up and realize that you are just like them. And God will deal with you the same as he dealt with them." The Israelites suddenly realized that this farmer had set them up. "For three sins of Israel, even for four, I will not turn back my wrath," he [God] says. "They sell the righteous for silver, and the needy for a pair of sandals. They trample on the heads of the poor as upon the dust of the ground and deny justice to the oppressed. Father and son use the same girl and so profane my holy name. They lie down beside every altar on garments taken in pledge. In the house of their god they drink wine taken as fines" (2:6–8).

In verse 13 Amos uses a marvelous image that only a farmer would employ: "Now then, [says the Lord] I will crush you as a cart crushes when loaded with grain."

God is saying, "Israel, you object to what people are doing in surrounding areas, but you are basically doing the same. You recognize that they deserve the judgment of God. But if they do, so do you!" Israel was no better than its neighbors. And Amos is promising them that God's judgment will come upon them. Their whole system is about to collapse like a cart overloaded with sacks of grain. This is the gist of his eight burdens.

Three Sermons

Now we will look briefly at the three sermons in Amos. The first one begins in chapter 3: "Hear this word the Lord has spoken against you, O people of Israel—against the whole family I brought up out of Egypt: 'You only have I chosen of all the families of the earth; therefore I will punish you for all your sins.' " This is a simple and straightforward sermon for God's covenant people. Jehovah, first of all, reminds Israel of their privileged position. Then he reiterates something that privileged people rarely want to hear. Special privilege always involves added responsibility.

" 'You only,' " he says, " 'Have I chosen of all the families of the earth. . . .' " That does not mean that Israel is exempt from judgment; rather, God says, because you are a people uniquely chosen to be my people, you qualify for judgment. "For it is time for judgment to begin with the family of God . . ." wrote Peter (1 Peter 4:17). Jesus said, "From everyone who has been given much, much will be demanded . . ." (Luke 12:48). Amos is telling Israel to rejoice in their privileged position, but to remember an important fact.

Their privilege does not exempt them from the judgment of God. Rather, because they have been particularly privileged, they are going to be uniquely responsible.

You who read Amos's book are privileged people. Think of it! Because you have read God's message you have been uniquely privileged, and you are overwhelmingly responsible. It is incumbent upon you to become more sensitive to what is wrong in the world than you were before. You need to become more disciplined than you were before. This is the way it was with the nation of Israel—because they were uniquely privileged, they were uniquely responsible.

In the sermon, Amos underlines an important truth: "The Sovereign Lord does nothing without revealing his plan to his servants, the prophets" (3:7). Because the Lord had revealed imminent judgment to Amos, he was responsible to tell Israel. Responsible people face up to God's expectations of them and take seriously his evaluation of their lives. Through Amos, God was warning his people of his evaluation, to give them time to come to repentance. "You have ample evidence of your privilege," Amos is saying. "You've had ample evidence that God is going to intervene in judgment. You still have time to repent. Hear the word of the Lord," he pleads, "Hear the word of the Lord."

Amos's second sermon begins: "Hear this word, you cows of Bashan on Mount Samaria, you women who oppress the poor and crush the needy and say to your husbands, 'Bring us some drinks!' " (Amos 4:1). I have already pointed out that Amos preaches like a farmer. Now note the way he addresses the ladies. He calls them, "You cows of Bashan. . . ." That's a farmer preaching! It is obvious that he hasn't been to seminary. He hasn't been taught how to put a sermon together, but he certainly gets their attention!

Amos goes on to point out God's utter disgust at their behavior, his total disdain for their hypocrisy. They are going on with all their external activities. On the outside they are living prosperous, sophisticated, absolutely magnificent lives, but underneath their hearts are far from God. They are utterly careless about real concerns. The practical outreach of their religion is nonexistent. God will not tolerate their irresponsible behavior any longer. " 'I gave you empty stomachs in every city and lack of bread in every town,' " he says, " 'yet you have not returned to me' " (v. 6). He points out, " 'People staggered from town to town for water but did not get enough to drink, yet you have not returned to me' " (v. 8). In verses 9, 10, and 11 he repeats this refrain: " 'yet you have not returned to me.' "

Amos must believe in repetition. He strings out one illustration after another to these sophisticated and perfumed women, living lives of luxury. They are the country-club ladies of Israel. They are having their special events, but underneath they are miles away from God. They have no real concern for people even though God has spoken to them repeatedly. He has intervened in their affairs. But while they would continue with their external sophistication, one thing they would not do; they would not return to the Lord.

After striving mightily to get their attention, Amos finally says, "Folks, you had better get your act together." Amos spells it out for them: " 'Therefore this is what I will do to you, Israel, and because I will do this to you, prepare to meet your God, O Israel' " (v. 12).

Cartoonists have lampooned this message by drawing pictures of a funny little old man carrying a poster. On it is written, "Prepare to meet your God!" That is probably one of the favorite targets of cartoonists. It says something about people's respect for the Word of God. But God is no joke! This God is awesome and all-powerful, utterly committed to justice. "The Lord God Almighty is his name" (v. 13).

The third sermon is aimed at Israel. "Hear this word, O house of Israel, this lament I take up concerning you," God says through Amos (5:1). He then goes on to point out several things.

First of all, they seem to prefer the externals of religion, but they refuse to seek a relationship with the Lord himself. In verses 4 and 5 he repeats, " 'Seek me and live. . . . Seek the Lord and live.' " In verse 14 he says, " 'Seek good, not evil, that you may live. Then the Lord God Almighty will be with you, just as you say he is.' " These people of Israel were happy to go into their worship places, but Jehovah was not the Lord of their lives.

In verse 18 Amos says, "Woe to you who long for the day of the Lord! Why do you long for the day of the Lord? That day will be darkness, not light." These people were so impressed with themselves and with their religion, they were looking for the day of the Lord, expecting all the blessing of heaven to shower upon them. God is saying in effect, "Why are you excited about the day of the Lord? It will not be a day of light for you; it will be a day of judgment."

Then Amos the farmer comes up with one of his magnificent metaphors: "It will be as though a man fled from a lion only to meet a bear, as though he entered his house and rested his hand on the wall only to have a snake bite him." Amos might not be a seminary graduate, but he surely knows how to use illustrations!

" 'I hate, I despise your religious feasts; I cannot stand your assemblies. Even though you bring me burnt offerings and grain offerings, I will not accept them. Though you bring choice fellowship offerings, I will have no regard for them. Away with the noise of your songs! I will not listen to the music of your harps' " (vv. 21–23). That is God's evaluation of their worship service.

What happens in our worship services? Do we sing to the Lord? Some of us don't bother singing—and some of us shouldn't! Some come just to look around. Others don't even arrive on time to sing to the Lord. I wonder if God ever critiques our worship services, if he is ever inclined to say to us, " 'Away with the noise of your songs!' "? Does he ever say, "I'm tired of the music of your harps"?

What God is really looking for is a people who have a heart for God, people who will stand for what God stands for. Amos concludes with a marvelous expression, and I'll conclude there as well: " 'But let justice roll on like a river and righteousness like a never-failing stream!' " (5:24).

Where there is reality, where people are not just going through the motions, the people will have a heart that stands for what God stands for. Justice and righteousness will be seen in our everyday lives. Instead of complacency, there will be commitment. That is the message Amos is trying to convey, and it is the message I leave with you now. God has spoken. Have you been listening?

F o u r
THE KINGDOM WILL BE THE LORD'S
Obadiah

THE BOOK OF OBADIAH is the shortest in the Old Testament—
only twenty-one verses in length. The prophet is speaking
out against Edom, Israel's neighbor to the south. The Edomites were descendants of Esau, Jacob's brother, and were
the inveterate enemies of Israel. This is the prophet's message concerning Edom:

The vision of Obadiah.
This is what the Sovereign Lord says about Edom—

We have heard a message from the Lord:
An envoy was sent to the nations to say,
"Rise, and let us go against her for battle"—

"See, I will make you small among the nations;
you will be utterly despised.
The pride of your heart has deceived you,
you who live in the clefts of the rocks

and make your home on the heights,
you who say to yourself, 'Who can bring me down
  to the ground?'
Though you soar like the eagle
and make your nest among the stars,
from there I will bring you down," declares the Lord.

"If thieves came to you, if robbers in the night—
Oh, what a disaster awaits you—
would they not steal only as much as they wanted?
If grape pickers came to you,
would they not leave a few grapes?
But how Esau will be ransacked,
his hidden treasures pillaged!
All your allies will force you to the border;
your friends will deceive and overpower you;
those who eat your bread will set a trap for you,
but you will not detect it.

"In that day," declares the Lord,
"will I not destroy the wise men of Edom,
men of understanding in the mountains of Esau?
Your warriors, O Teman, will be terrified,
and everyone in Esau's mountains
will be cut down in the slaughter.
Because of the violence against your brother Jacob,
you will be covered with shame;
you will be destroyed forever.
On the day you stood aloof while strangers carried off
  his wealth
and foreigners entered his gates
and cast lots for Jerusalem, you were like one of them.
You should not look down on your brother
in the day of his misfortune,
nor rejoice over the people of Judah
in the day of their destruction,
nor boast so much in the day of their trouble.
You should not march

through the gates of my people
in the day of their disaster,
nor look down on them in their calamity
   in the day of their disaster,
nor seize their wealth in the day of their disaster.
You should not wait at the crossroads
to cut down their fugitives,
nor hand over their survivors
in the day of their trouble.

The day of the Lord is near
   for all nations.
As you have done, it will be done to you;
your deeds will return upon your own head."

(vv. 1–15)

Obadiah prophesied in the time of Jeremiah and Ezekiel, but little is known of his personal history. He lived more than five hundred years before the time of Christ, but we do not know the exact dates of his lifetime.

What a bleak picture Obadiah paints of Edom, a group of people closely related in language and blood to the Israelites. But the tone changes in verse 17 where the prophet promises, " 'But on Mount Zion will be deliverance. . . .' " The prophecy then concludes with these words, "Deliverers will go up on Mount Zion to govern the mountains of Esau. And the kingdom will be the Lord's" (v. 21).

In our society today there is a tremendous emphasis on human rights. It almost seems that we are interested in God only to the extent to which he will benefit mankind. Rarely do we come across people who are God-centered in their outlook. Rather, we most often encounter those who are man-centered in their perspective. These people regard man as the central fact of the universe. Even those who claim to be the Lord's, who acknowledge the Lord as Savior, often give the unfortunate impression that they take God seriously only when it suits them. Most of the time they seem to put the things of the world, material things, higher on their scale of priorities.

There is no question that God takes himself seriously. There's equally no question but that he expected the prophets to take him seriously. I do not doubt, either, that when the prophet spoke he expected his hearers to take God seriously. That is why it is particularly timely to study what the ancient prophets had to say, because what they proclaimed is strikingly applicable to this present day.

The early church father, Jerome, claimed that the difficulties associated with Obadiah were in inverse proportion to its size. However, I do not intend to deal with the problems. Rather, I want us to look at the message. Obadiah is assuring us that the authoritative rule of God in the affairs of men is to be counted on and reckoned with. This must be understood. Finally and irrevocably, as Obadiah puts it, the kingdom will be the Lord's. That is the crystal clear message of this rather obscure little book.

The Meaning of Obadiah's Name

The first thing we notice in this prophecy is the emphasis on his name. Obadiah literally means "one who serves or worships Jehovah." This prophecy, though it is against Edom, is given to the people of Judah. Picture, if you will, a map of the Dead Sea. From the Dead Sea, go in a southeasterly direction, and you will be traveling through some of the wildest, most barren territory on the face of the earth. This is the ancient land of Edom, the area where Esau settled.

Obadiah's prophecy against Edom is simply this: Several nations have formed a coalition of states, united in their opposition to Israel. Interestingly enough, Obadiah makes it clear that Jehovah-God is involved in Edom's downfall; he is busily engaged behind the scenes. As Obadiah says, "This is what the Sovereign Lord says about Edom. . . ."

The Hand of God

We notice two important things immediately from the prophecy of Obadiah. First, Obadiah recognizes the hand of God at work in the military and political lives of these neighbors of Judah. It may seem surprising that God would be at work in the affairs of Edom, and those of its Arab neighbors around Edom, in order to carry out his purposes. Obadiah is pointing out a truth that we must never forget or overlook: The Sovereign Lord is building his kingdom, using some unlikely tools to carry out his plan.

It is possible sometimes to see the hand of the Sovereign Lord at work in the military build-ups and political movements and machinations of the age in which we live. As believers, we must not look at these military build-ups in the Middle East as some people do. It would be wrong for believers to view such things from a political perspective alone. If we Christians believe that the Lord is Sovereign, that he is moving inexorably toward the ultimate and final establishment of his eternal kingdom, we must have an entirely different view of the developments in our world. If this was true of Edom and the nations surrounding it at the time of Obadiah, we have good cause for believing that the same is true today.

I become alarmed sometimes at the political involvement of many believers today in matters totally unrelated to their theology. I'm not suggesting that because we are spiritual people we have no time for politics, or no interest whatsoever in international affairs. That attitude is quite regrettable. But at the same time, it is out of order for Christians to take a political position more related to their tradition and economic status than to their theology. It is absolutely imperative for us to recognize that theology comes first: We must understand who the Sovereign Lord is and recognize that he is building his kingdom. Whatever our political persuasions might be, they must be in harmony with the principles of the kingdom of God. We must watch the events taking place in our world and be deeply concerned about them, but we must remember that as we see important events developing around us, the kingdom will be the Lord's. In all that is happening, the Sovereign Lord is working out his purposes.

This Sovereign Lord is speaking through Obadiah to the people of Edom. He is not at all reluctant to tell them that plain, unadulterated judgment is on its way. He is not at all hesitant or apologetic about it. Edom is facing the judgment of God. It will come in the form of a military overthrow, at the hands of their Arab neighbors. Regardless of the consequences, the judgment is coming. Notice this, however: Before judgment comes, ample warning is given. This is always the divine principle.

We are seeing as we study the prophets these two basic aspects of the divine character: 1) the holy, righteous God will judge where judgment is necessary, and 2) the gracious, merciful, loving God will always warn of impending judgment. He will be patient and longsuffering to give people time to repent. This is the background behind Obadiah's prophecy. The situation in Edom is seen from Judah's perspective.

The second thing we notice in Obadiah is the nature of Jehovah's action through this Arab coalition against Edom. In verse 2 he warns that Edom will suffer a catastrophic defeat: " 'See, I will make you small among the nations; you will be utterly despised.' "

The people of Edom had a right to be proud. Though they dwelt in a forbidding and desolate area, they had managed to establish themselves quite firmly. God says, however, "Even though you are a powerful force your days are numbered. Your kingdom will be overthrown and you will be seen by all around you to have come under the judgment of God."

The Lord Is in Control

All the great kingdoms and empires have sooner or later crumbled and fallen into the dust. This is, of course, a reminder that the Sovereign Lord is in control. There have been kings and there have been dictators. There have been emperors and Caesars. Their kingdoms have come and gone. These rulers have one thing in common. Their bones now mold in obscure graves, but the Sovereign Lord rules. God is still on the throne.

Never forget this fact. Where are the great kingdoms? Where are the great empires? Where are the great forces resident in the world today? If God should tarry, there is one thing we can depend upon. They, too, will crumble. If God should tarry, those who vaunt themselves, those who are proud, those who congratulate themselves on their own greatness will hear God say, "I will make you small among the nations."

Some years ago I was talking to Ruth Bell Graham. She had just been reading about the moral conditions in the United States, and I will never forget what she said to me. "When I read all this data concerning the moral disintegration of the United States of America," she said, "I think that if God does not bring judgment upon the United States one day he will have to apologize to Sodom and Gomorrah." A catastrophic defeat awaits all those who vaunt themselves against the Sovereign Lord, who will not order their lives according to his principles, and there are no exceptions to this principle.

Notice also that total economic deprivation was coming. Obadiah puts it in poetic language, " 'If thieves came to you, if robbers in the night . . . would they not steal only as much as they wanted? If grape pickers came to you, would they not leave a few grapes? But how Esau will be ransacked, his hidden treasures pillaged!' " (vv. 5, 6).

Esau is, of course, a synonym for Edom. Obadiah is saying that Edom is going to be totally and utterly wiped out. In verse 7 he says that those whom they had formerly regarded as their allies will fail them: "All your allies will force you to the border; your friends will deceive and overpower you; those who eat your bread will set a trap for you, but you will not detect it." In other words, all their former alliances will come to nothing. All their alliances, covenants, and agreements will be callously broken. As a result of this judgment, the structures of their society will begin to collapse.

" 'In that day,' declares the Lord, 'will I not destroy the wise men of Edom, men of understanding in the mountains of Esau? Your warriors, O Teman, will be terrified, and everyone in Esau's mountains will be cut down in the slaughter' " (v. 8). The whole structure is going to come crashing down. Notice this—a military defeat, an economic collapse, the disintegration of the principles of society, and the breaking of political alliances are all interpreted as being the judgment of God. According to Obadiah, these are the clear-cut judgment of God.

People sometimes disregard the idea of God's judgment. If they consider God as judging at all, they are usually thinking of a final and awesome day of judgment. But the Scriptures are very clear. God moves in the affairs of nations and sits in judgment upon wrongdoers. Certainly in this instance, and many other times in the Old Testament, we see his judgment coming down in very practical terms. The Bible is clear: "Do not be deceived: God cannot be mocked. A man [or a nation!] reaps what he sows" (Gal. 6:7). Paul here was simply echoing what Obadiah had already said: "The day of the Lord is near for all nations. As you have done, it will be done to you; your deeds will return upon your own head" (v. 15).

Edom is facing God's judgment. What are the reasons for this action?

First of all, arrogance. " 'The pride of your heart has deceived you,' " says Obadiah, " 'you who live in the clefts of the rocks and make your home on the heights, you who say to yourself, "Who can bring me down to the ground?" ' " Their arrogant self-sufficiency has been so deep and so ingrained in their thinking that these Edomites, many scholars think, were almost unique. You can go anywhere in the world and you will find that people have gods of some kind to whom they swear allegiance and upon whom they claim dependence. But scholars say that for the Edomites they find no record or statement of any kind of dependence at all. The Edomites had no allegiance to a god. This has led many scholars to believe that this unusual people were so self-sufficient, arrogant, and self-satisfied that they wouldn't even call upon the name of any kind of god. They believed they had all the answers themselves!

This was one of God's primary complaints against them. Remember what God said through Daniel to Belshazzar? A hand appeared, writing something on the wall. We still commemorate that event when we use the expression "the handwriting on the wall." The handwriting simply predicted judgment upon Belshazzar and Babylon. Daniel was offered all kinds of money if he could interpret the king's dream. But Daniel said, "Forget it. You can keep your money, but I will interpret the dream for you. And the dream is very simply this, your majesty. Your days are numbered; you have had it. This is why. Your father was as arrogant and self-sufficient and opposed to God as you are— and you know what happened to your father. God humbled him so that he might come to grips with the reality of himself and the reality of God. Your father had the sense to learn from his humbling circumstances. But you, King Belshazzar, with that model before you, have gone on in the arrogant ways of your father. You have not learned from his experience, and you have refused to glorify God in whose hand is your very breath! Therefore, Belshazzar, you will be brought down" (see Daniel 5).

God says, "Pride do I hate!" He makes it very clear that the first sin was the sin of that proud angel who decided he was going to be equal with God. God will not tolerate that kind of pride in an individual, a group, or a nation. Such self-sufficiency says, "I can make it without God; I don't need God; I don't want God; God is irrelevant." That attitude, sooner or later, merits the judgment of God. That judgment will come.

A False Sense of Security

Edom's arrogant attitude, their self-sufficiency, brought them to a state of misplaced security.

Centuries later, the particular area where the Edomites lived was overrun by the Nabateans. These people built one of the most remarkable cities known in the history of mankind, the city of Petra. If you have the opportunity to visit Petra, you should do it; it is a long and difficult journey, but worth every unpleasantness.

To reach Petra, one descends a steep, rocky incline through a narrow, tunnel-like gully. Once inside the city, the visitor can see what a remarkably secure military position it enjoyed. All the buildings of Petra have been carved out of solid red stone. The city has some magnificent temples and sophisticated buildings. It is unbelievable what these people did in building Petra, and it is easy to see why the citizenry felt that their citadel was impregnable. But impregnable Petra now lies in ruins.

But remember, Isaiah said, "Woe to those who . . . trust in horses, who trust in the multitude of their chariots and in the great strength of their horsemen . . ." (31:1). It is better to put one's trust in the Lord, because in the final analysis, the kingdom will be the Lord's. If Obadiah's prophecy tells us anything, it is that those who are proud will fall, those who exalt themselves will be humbled by God, those who trust in their own strength and might will eventually come crashing down.

Worldly Wisdom

The Edomites were lulled into complacency by their worldly intellectualism. Their wisdom was a byword in their day. They had no interest in building wisdom based on the revelation of God himself.

If these people were living in such an isolated region, you ask, how come they were so wise? They were isolated, but being situated close to the crossroads of the great trade routes, they had all the contact they wanted with everyone coming from east and west. Thus, they had acquired for themselves the wisdom of this world. And their worldly wisdom ruled out any dependence upon God.

Edom's animosity toward God goes back to the father of the Edomites, Esau. The Bible frequently refers to the longstanding feud between Esau and Jacob and their descendants. It makes some of our modern-day family and international feuds look like peace meetings!

Look at some of the details of this feud. Jacob and Esau were twins, and they even fought each other in their mother's womb. Even as they came out of the womb they were struggling together. There was considerable antipathy between them as they grew up. Later, as the children of Israel (or Jacob) left Egypt for the Promised Land, they had to pass through Edom. They went to the people of Edom and asked for permission to pass through, promising to be on their good behavior and to repair any damage they might do. But Edom would not let them through. In fact, they attacked the Israelites and were continually hostile toward them (see Ezekiel 35, Jeremiah 49:7–22, and Psalm 137:7).

The violent antipathy between Edom and the people and purposes of God reached a climax in one of the most dramatic confrontations of all time—when Jesus stood before King Herod. As Jesus stood there, Herod wanted Jesus to give him a sample of his preaching. But Jesus gave him nothing but a loud silence. Jesus had earlier been warned of Herod and called the king "that fox," indicating the unscrupulous character of the man. Herod was an Idumean, or Edomite. When the Nabateans took over their territory, the descendants of Esau went into the land south of Judea and there became known as Idumeans. Herod typified the longstanding, unrelenting antipathy toward God on the part of the Edomites (Idumeans).

We should always remember this: The judgment of God will inevitably fall on arrogant, self-sufficient, self-confident, worldly-wise people who rule out God and oppose his purposes. Why? Because the kingdom will be the Lord's.

A Dramatic Contrast

Now notice how this prophecy ends, and what it has in common with other prophecies in the Bible. The prophets come with their pronunciations of doom and judgment, and the people don't like to hear that kind of message. However, all the prophets end on a note of hope. God's message has an "up" side as well as a "down" side. He is a God of justice and righteousness who must judge the ungodly, but he is also a God of love and mercy who longs to bless the repentant.

In marked contrast to the fate of Edom, there is a dramatic promise concerning Israel's future: "But on Mount Zion will be deliverance . . . the house of Jacob will possess its inheritance" (v. 17). The prophets thought in terms of the Promised Land. They thought in terms of the city of Jerusalem, particularly that part of the city called Mount Zion, the temple area. On Mount Zion there will be deliverance.

Scholars have difficulty pinpointing the exact date of Obadiah's prophecy, but I'm inclined to think the time referred to is after Nebuchadnezzar destroyed Jerusalem in 587 B.C. If that is the case, Obadiah is speaking to people already in captivity. In all probability he is saying, "You people in captivity remember this. Edom looks as if it is triumphant right now. But don't forget, God says Edom will come crumbling down and you who are apparently defeated will possess your possessions."

I think Obadiah is predicting the restoration of the people in exile, telling them they are going back to their land, their city, and the temple.

He goes on to say, " 'The house of Jacob will be a fire and the house of Joseph a flame; the house of Esau will be stubble, and they will set it on fire and consume it. There will be no survivors from the house of Esau' " (v. 18). An interesting thing happened as far as the Edomites were concerned. The Nabateans threw them out of their area, and they moved into the south of Judea. Later, in 125 B.C., the Edomites (or Idumeans) were overthrown and they lost their nationhood and identity. They lost their uniqueness and to all intents and purposes disappeared. If you travel today in the region of Edom, you will find nothing but the most stark wilderness and the most isolated emptiness. Petra is one of the most formidable, forsaken spots on earth.

In marked contrast, what happened to God's people? There is no question about it: Edom was destroyed, but Israel was restored. The fate of Israel was in dramatic contrast to the fate of Edom. One lesson comes through loud and clear: God is sovereign; he is in charge. When he speaks the word that the time of judgment has come, nothing will stop him. When he makes a commitment to bless and to restore, he will do so. Succinctly put, that is the message of Obadiah. It is a message that illustrates for us in dramatic language and historically-verifiable facts that the Lord is sovereign and that the kingdom will be the Lord's.

Summing It All Up

What are the lessons for us?

First of all, God works out his purposes in the actions and affairs of mankind. We can look at the world around us, at the activities of mankind and nations, and we can either believe that man has his destiny in his own hands and God is irrelevant, or we can accept God as sovereign and working in these affairs. That is our monumental decision; it is the very basis of our world view. I believe either that I have my destiny in my own hands—and God is sitting on the sidelines wringing his hands, bemoaning his irrelevance—or I believe that the Sovereign Lord is really ruling and working. If I believe the Old Testament prophets, I have reason to believe God when he says he will do certain things. Is God trying to tell me something? Is God trying to tell me in history that he is sovereign, that he rules in the affairs of men and that he utilizes the actions of man to bring about his eternal purposes? That is a decision I have to make.

A second lesson: Pride always comes before a fall. "Whom the Father loves, he chastens." One of the hardest things for a parent to do is to allow a cocky, impudent little son who has grown too big for his boots to fall flat on his face. But sometimes that is what must be done. If that little upstart doesn't learn when he is little, unfortunately he will have to learn when he is big—sometimes behind bars! If he thinks he has all the answers and knows everything, then sooner or later (sooner is best!) he must learn humility. This principle obtains in parenting little children and guiding teenagers, in building solid marriage relationships, in business situations, and in the spiritual life.

If we insist on our own greatness, we eventually will have to be cut down to size, because we were created to be dependent on our Creator. If we think we have it all together, we could not be more wrong—and the sooner we learn it the better. That is why God tells us, "If you will humble yourself under my mighty hand, I will exalt you. But if you exalt yourself, I will humble you."

The final lesson is simply this: The King is building his kingdom and he will prevail.

So, there is one question and it is this: If the Lord is sovereign and if the kingdom will be the Lord's, is the King *your* King? Is the King *my* King? Are you part of his kingdom?

To put it another way, when the day of the Lord eventually comes, will you bow the knee joyfully to the King because it has become a matter of habit all the days of your life? Will you greet him with great joy? Or will you fall in utter terror before the King because you know your day of judgment is coming? The glorious truth of the matter is this: The awful wrath of God against sin fell on Christ at the cross. Men and women who recognize their sin can turn to Christ and ask God for Christ's sake to forgive them. Repentance and faith will lead inevitably to blessing. Arrogant, hard-hearted self-sufficiency based on wordly wisdom will lead inevitably to judgment for the individual and the nation. What will it be for you—the joy of Jesus, or the judgment of God?

F i v e

THE KINDNESS OF GOD
Jonah

THE BOOK OF JONAH—the only autobiographical work among the twelve minor prophets—is as controversial as it is popular. Some people would judge a person's orthodoxy by his attitude toward Jonah. "If you don't believe literally all the details of this particular story, then it is highly unlikely that you are a Christian," they would say. They reason that since the Lord Jesus used the story of Jonah as an illustration of his own death and resurrection, we must take this story literally. Jesus obviously believed it literally, they point out, and if you don't, there's a question about your faith!

Others note that Jesus told parables and Paul used allegory. They ask: "Does it make any difference in the truth expressed? Surely the Old Testament has as many means of communicating truth as does the New Testament, does it not?"

To judge a person's biblical or evangelical orthodoxy by his attitude toward the literalness of this story may be rather presumptuous. Let's face it. Scholarly evangelical Christians disagree on how to approach this particular story. Some are extremely adamant. It must be read as a specific historical document. Others would say, no, it is a parable, and it should be understood in this light. Still others insist it is an allegory, meaning that various aspects of the story stand for different things and can be applied to different things. John Bunyan's *Pilgrim's Progress* is the classic example of allegory.

Suffice it to say that sometimes we read the Word of God and miss the whole point of it because we are looking at the wrong things or we are fighting at the wrong places.

A Great Fish or a Great God?

It seems to me as we look at Jonah that we should remember what a great Bible teacher of a past generation said. G. Campbell Morgan wisely pointed out, "Men have been looking so hard at the great fish that they have failed to see the great God." In this particular story we should not put all our attention on the great fish. Rather, Jonah's story is designed to draw our attention to the great God who is revealed to us through the inspiration of the Holy Spirit. We should focus our attention on him! Of course, as we look at Jonah we are confronted with some remarkable things. The most remarkable thing in the minds of many people is the statement that God provided a great fish. Notice, it does not say he provided a whale. God provided a great fish. People say, "Do you really want us to believe that Jonah was swallowed and was three days and three nights in the belly of a fish?"

Others have pointed out that there is a much bigger miracle in this story than a fish swallowing Jonah. The greatest miracle, they say, is that the whole of Nineveh repented at the preaching of Jonah! If you read the whole book you find that God provided not just a fish, but all kinds of

things! He provided a fish, he provided the wind, he provided the vine—he even provided a worm!

The Kindness of God

As we look into the portrayal of God in this story, it is
obvious to me that the aspect of God's character the writer
is most concerned to project is his *kindness*. God calls Jonah
the prophet and says to him, " 'Go to the great city of
Nineveh and preach against it, because its wickedness has
come up before me' " (1:2).

First of all, notice that God's kindness is demonstrated
in the fact that he is concerned about and is prepared to
send his prophet to a noncovenant people. The covenant people of Israel had carefully overlooked the fact that
Jehovah-God cared for other people.

From the beginning God had said quite categorically that
he was going to call Abraham to himself, and that the children of Abraham (and subsequently the children of Israel)
would be his special people. Israel latched on to that. They
were thrilled about the covenant God had made with them,
and the responsive covenant they had made with God. But
one thing they had consistently, carefully overlooked. God
had promised that through his covenant people all the nations of the earth would be blessed. Israel was not interested
in that. Though they had become exclusive in their thinking, God is showing them here, through the prophet Jonah,
that his kindness embraces not only those who are a part
of his covenant people, but, through them, those also who
are not.

God's kindness is also demonstrated by his concern for
a people who are utterly corrupt. The people of Nineveh
are described as those whose "wickedness" had come up
before him. God decides that their wickedness needs to
be confronted.

Notice something further. The kindness of God is exhibited through the call of Jonah. Jonah is called, not only
to go to a noncovenant, totally corrupt people; he is called

to *warn* them of what is going to happen. This needs to be underlined. Some think it is kind not to confront people when they are wrong. Sometimes it is desperately unkind *not* to do so. There is a time to speak out and take a stand against the wrong in our world. We sometimes show the depth and degree of our concern, our compassion, and our kindness for people by standing up and speaking against what they are doing.

God's kindness is also exhibited through his desire to approach the people and get to them *where they are.* It was not uncommon to find the prophets of Israel and Judah speaking out against the surrounding nations from within the security of Palestine's own borders. We saw how Amos did this. But Jonah is an exception. He is told to go to the center of Nineveh and there stand up and preach against the sin of the people. God is not remote and uncaring. He involves himself with them; he gets right to them where they are. Thus we see the kindness of God being exhibited to the people of Nineveh through his call to Jonah to go to them.

The Disobedient Prophet

What happened next? Jonah, having been called and commissioned to go to Nineveh, promptly boards a ship heading in exactly the opposite direction! He heads for Tarshish, situated at the western end of the Mediterranean—as far from Nineveh as he knew to go. We don't know whether he went down and jumped on any old ship that was going anywhere—or if he asked his local travel agent for the most westerly point, as far as possible from Nineveh! We *do* know that the contrary prophet went in exactly the opposite direction he was told to go.

But notice how God's care for Jonah exhibits his kindness to the people of Nineveh. God pursued his disobedient prophet. He didn't just let him go. Jehovah enlisted all the natural forces to change Jonah's course, and thereby demonstrated that he, in his almighty power, is prepared to bring all his considerable resources to bear on the life of the individual.

How kind can God be? He actually caused a storm to center in on the boat to bring Jonah to his senses. We can use the expression: God is ready to move heaven and earth to get his message through to those who turn their backs on him.

Notice also that God in his considerable kindness surrounded Jonah with noble pagans. The people who were handling the ship exhibit considerable insight and sensitivity. How kind they are to this man who has brought all sorts of problems on them. They even demonstrate a remarkable openness to Jonah's God. After they finished what they felt they ought to do, the Bible tells us, they "greatly feared the Lord" (see v. 16). They even "offered a sacrifice to the Lord and made vows to him."

God is not prepared to cast off this rascally prophet even though he deserves it! Not only does God surround him with noble pagans; he challenges the disobedient prophet to remember the things that he professes to believe. Notice the questions the sailors ask: " 'What do you do? Where do you come from? What is your country? From what people are you?' " (v. 8). Answer: " 'I am a Hebrew and I worship the Lord, the God of heaven, who made the sea and the land.' " What purpose did the sailors serve in Jonah's life? They forced the bitter prophet to reflect upon his faith. God kindly puts him in a situation where he is being reminded of the things he professes to believe.

I've noticed this about God. When we are the most distant from him, the hounds of heaven keep pursuing us. So often we wish God would leave us alone, but in his unspeakable kindness he refuses to do so. A friend of mine, and fellow minister, went through this experience some time ago. For three years he willfully turned his back on God. Though he had been deeply involved in the ministry, he became discouraged and disgruntled and turned his back on the church and on God. This is what he told me: "For three years, I lived in self-imposed exile from God; never a day went by without my being convicted in the depth of my soul that I was wrong." God was very kind to that man who is now back in the midst of a very effective ministry.

God's *care* for Jonah as well as his *call* to Jonah exhibits his kindness. As Jonah was being dispatched over the side of the boat, God provided a unique submersible vehicle for him to ride in. Even in the midst of Jonah's rebellion, God continued to care for his prophet. That is why I see the theme of Jonah as "the kindness of God." This theme dominates the whole of chapter 1.

The Psalm of Jonah

Chapter 2 is a psalm and a prayer that Jonah prayed to the Lord "from inside the fish." People raise the question: "Do you really want us to believe that this guy in the middle of a fish is composing poetry?" As thinking people, we all struggle with such a question. Whatever our feeling is here, we must not forget that the Book of Jonah is a statement concerning the kindness of God. In this chapter it is apparent that Jonah is beginning to recognize God's kindness—and he makes a powerful statement concerning it. Jonah's psalm is a reflection upon his own behavior as well as God's goodness:

"In my distress I called to the Lord,
    and he answered me.
From the depths of the grave
I called for help,
    and you listened to my cry.
You hurled me into the deep,
    into the very heart of the seas,
    and the currents swirled about me;
    all your waves and breakers swept over me.
I said, 'I have been banished from your sight;
yet I will look again toward your holy temple.'
The engulfing waters threatened me,
    the deep surrounded me;

seaweed was wrapped around my head.
To the roots of the mountains I sank down;
   the earth beneath barred me in forever.
But you brought my life up from the pit,
   O Lord my God.
When my life was ebbing away,
   I remembered you, Lord,
and my prayer rose to you,
   to your holy temple.
Those who cling to worthless idols
   forfeit the grace that could be theirs.
But I, with a song of thanksgiving,
   will sacrifice to you.
What I have vowed I will make good.
   Salvation comes from the Lord." (2:2–9)

Jonah had the opportunity to reflect on the things that he had done. He began to see in those things the thread of God's faithfulness and concern, a hint of his compassion. Jonah also reviewed God's dramatic intervention in his life. Of course, he could not overlook that even as the engulfing waters threatened him and the deep surrounded him—the "seaweed was wrapped around [his] head"—even then, he said, ". . . you brought my life up from the pit."

Many of us today could testify that though we might not have been in the belly of a whale, we have been down in the depths. We may not have had the seaweed wrapped around our heads, but we have found ourselves in real difficulty. Yet as we look back over those experiences we can review God's kind and gracious intervention in our lives.

Notice another fact about this particular psalm. According to those who have studied it carefully, it is not very original. Rather, it seems to be a compilation of the innumerable thoughts expressed in other psalms. By this I am saying that as Jonah wrote this specific psalm perhaps many of the psalms he had read came to his remembrance. That is the work of the Spirit in his life. Remember this, however. You cannot remember what you don't already know. In his kindness through the Holy Spirit, God is committed to bringing to our remembrance at our darkest hours the truth that will shed light on our situation. But we must have taken the trouble to learn that truth for ourselves. Even the Holy Spirit cannot bring to remembrance what we don't already know!

Many people can testify that at the moment of their greatest extremity, the Spirit of God reminded them of the deep things of God. They have been confronted and encouraged. How good God is, Jonah is reminded, and he sings: "But I, with a song of thanksgiving, will sacrifice to you. What I have vowed I will make good. Salvation comes from the Lord." Jonah's attitude has undergone a dramatic transformation. As he recognizes God's kindness, he experiences this change of heart. Always remember the powerful statement of the New Testament that the kindness and goodness of God lead us to repentance (see Romans 2:4).

I remember when our daughter Judy came as close to rebelling as any of our children ever did. She was having a difficult time and things were pretty tense between her and my wife Jill. Although nothing was terribly out of hand, it was a matter for concern and prayer. Judy was babysitting for another couple, and she called home to talk to Jill. "Mom," she said, "I need to talk to you." Jill, of course, always assumes the worst and she knew that either the house was on fire or there was a burglar—or both. So she asked, "What's the matter?"

"Nothing is really the matter," Judy replied. "I just need to say I'm sorry."

"About what?" Jill asked.

"About me and my attitude," Judy said.

"Judy, why are you suddenly calling me from two or three blocks away to tell me this?" Jill exclaimed.

"Because I can't leave it unsaid any longer," Judy answered.

Jill paused a moment, then asked, "Judy, why is it that now you want to say you are sorry and to put things right?"

"Because I have been sitting here reflecting on your kindness," Judy replied. (And she didn't know she was quoting the Bible.) Then she went on, "It is your kindness that has led me to say I'm sorry."

It is the kindness, the goodness of God that leads us to repentance. Even Jonah, crusty old rascal of a prophet that he was, recognized this. In him we see a delightful picture of God's kindness taking hold in a person's life.

God's Kindness to Nineveh

In the third chapter, we see more of God's kindness, but now it is exhibited in his dealings with Nineveh. Many people, after they have repented, assume that things will quiet down and God will leave them alone. *"Whew,"* they say, *"that is a relief!* No more conviction. Oh, what a joy, everything is squared away with God! Now I will leave him alone if he will leave me alone." That is not what happens.

Chapter 3 begins with a remarkable statement: "Then the word of the Lord came to Jonah a second time: 'Go to the great city of Nineveh and proclaim to it the message I give you.'" In other words, God is saying to Jonah, "Get yourself sorted out. Go and do what I told you to do in the first place."

Why does God do this? Because he is totally committed to Nineveh. He is deeply serious about getting his message to the people of that city. Even though there have been all kinds of problems in the way, he is going to deal with Nineveh. We should not focus on Jonah here. Rather, we need to focus on God. In this story God is the star, the chief character—not Jonah.

What do we see here? We see the unrelenting persistence of God as far as this great city of Nineveh is concerned. Notice that Jonah finally agrees, very reluctantly, to go: "Jonah obeyed the word of the Lord and went to Nineveh. Now Nineveh was a very large city; it took three days to go all the way through it. Jonah started into the city, going a day's journey, and he proclaimed: 'Forty more days and Nineveh will be destroyed' " (vv. 3, 4).

What was Nineveh's response? They believed God!

It should be obvious that Jonah had more to say than just these eight words. What the biblical writer gives us is the thrust of his oracle. Why is it obvious that he had more to say than that? Because it is clear that Jonah proclaimed his message in the name of the Lord God and said all that God wanted him to. The people linked this prediction of disaster with the activity of God and they recognized that if disaster were to be averted, they would have to get right with God themselves. Jonah's statement is clearly a proclamation not only of the purpose of God but also of the nature and the character and the being of God.

God graciously revealed himself to the people of Nineveh. Have you ever pondered the sheer kindness of God in that he took the initiative and decided to let them (and us) know what he is like? What if God had not taken the initiative to reveal himself to us? Would we ever have known him? It is of the Lord's goodness and the Lord's kindness that we know anything of him at all.

I believe the Ninevites understood that. They were shattered not only by the prediction concerning what was going to happen to them, but also, they were overwhelmed by God's kindness in that he had sent his prophet, delivered the word to them, given them the opportunity to repent and then had dealt graciously with them.

Notice how they showed their response: "The Ninevites believed God." How do we know they believed God? "They declared a fast, and all of them, from the greatest to the least, put on sackcloth. When the news reached the king of Nineveh, he rose from his throne, took off his royal robes, covered himself with sackcloth and sat down in the dust. Then he issued a proclamation to Nineveh: '. . . Do not let any man or beast, herd or flock, taste anything; do not let them eat or drink. But let man and beast be covered with sackcloth. Let everyone call urgently on God.

Let them give up their evil ways and their violence. Who knows? God may yet relent and with compassion turn from his fierce anger so that we will not perish' " (vv. 5–9).

The people heard and believed God. They turned to the Lord and clearly exhibited the depth of their contrition and confession. They declared a fast, not only for themselves but for their domestic animals. All their gorgeous apparel they stripped away and put on uncomfortable, scratchy sackcloth to reflect the depth of their repentance from sin. The Ninevites turned to prayer and everyone was required to call urgently upon God.

Doesn't this remind you of what we noted in Joel's prophecy? There, everyone was required to come before the Lord in repentance and confession, and call urgently upon him. Absolutely everyone was required to do it. They were also required to turn away from their evil.

Notice, too, the particular emphasis on violence in the king's decree: "Let them give up their evil ways and their violence." This was one of the objectionable things about Nineveh. The people were unbelievably violent and loved strife. God told them to turn from this, and thus they recognized the sovereignty of God. They do not say, "If we do this we can manipulate God and he will have to be kind to us." Rather, the king said, "The very least we can do is all this. Who knows? God in his sovereignty may be kind to us."

These pagans had a remarkable handle on the truth of God, and of his self-revelation. As they respond to God's kindness, even more kindness is to come. God, having shown his kindness to Nineveh in his persistence in sending the prophet and revealing his purposes and his person, now demonstrates his kindness by turning from what he has said he will do.

Jeremiah 18:7–10 is the classic passage that illustrates how God can change his mind: "If at any time I announce that a nation or kingdom is to be uprooted, torn down and destroyed, and if that nation I warned repents of its evil, then I will relent and not inflict on it the disaster I had planned. And if at another time I announce that a nation or kingdom is to be built up and planted, and if it does evil in my sight and does not obey me, then I will reconsider the good I had intended to do for it." How illustrative this is of the way God dealt with Nineveh. God's almost unbelievable kindness to Nineveh is a picture of his gracious dealings with us.

Jonah's Anger

In the fourth and final chapter, we see God's kindness presented in an entirely different way. The Book of Jonah is a skillfully-crafted literary document. Here the kindness of God is demonstrated in the contrast between God's attitude and Jonah's. Jonah was really angry. He didn't want these people to repent, for he didn't want them to enjoy the blessings that the privileged few are supposed to receive. Even though he preached and the people repented, he turned to God and said in effect: "I told you so!" (see 4:2). "I knew they would repent," Jonah complains. "That's why I didn't come in the first place! I knew that if I preached they would repent and you would be kind and you would forgive them and they would have the privileges I enjoy— and I don't want them to have the privileges that I enjoy!"

Against that kind of attitude, it's easy to see the grace of God. Unfortunately, it is usually not difficult to see the grace and kindness of God in comparison with the lack of grace and kindness on the part of many of God's people. That's why this message from God is so powerful. As this prophecy was presented to the people of Israel, Jehovah showed them that in their attitudes they were very much like their spokesman, Jonah.

God's Attitude

In contrast to theirs, the attitude of God shows a wonderful concern. We need to be fair to Jonah here. He had had it with the Assyrians. The people of Israel were also "fed up" with the Assyrians. That nation had been violent and cruel toward Israel, thus Israel's bitterness was understandable. In my hometown in Great Britain there are many who are understandably bitter against the Japanese. A regiment from our town arrived in Singapore the very day that Singapore capitulated, so that all the men of a certain age group in my small hometown spent all of World War II in a Japanese POW camp.

I remember, however, going to Japan, and meeting there a man who is giving his life to minister to the Japanese. He is the strangest speaker I have ever heard in my life. His voice box had been shot out, so that he had no voice at all. A Japanese sniper had shot him as he went ashore on Okinawa, putting a bullet straight through his throat. Yet this man now demonstrates his response to the call of God to the Japanese people by giving himself to those people who shot him. Serving with The Navigators, he is one of the most remarkable missionaries I have ever met. If anyone has a right to be bitter, this man does. But instead, he loves his former enemies.

If anyone has a right and a reason to be bitter, God does. But God prefers to exhibit his kindness in the face of *our* bitterness. Against our bitterness the kindness of God is shown in sharp relief.

Jonah set up a little booth where he waits to see what is going to happen to Nineveh. He hopes that the Ninevites won't really repent. He wants them to be destroyed by God—but he has a deep-down sneaky feeling that God is going to be kind to them. This upsets him for he feels the Ninevites deserve God's wrath rather than his love.

What is God's point of view? He looks down at the crusty old prophet sitting there, getting a sunstroke, and he provides a vine for him. When the shade from the vine reaches Jonah, he is thrilled at what God has done. Then God provides the worm that chews on the vine—and the whole thing disintegrates. That makes Jonah even more angry!

Notice, however, that Jonah is not angry just because

his shade has been taken away; he is upset because this lovely little vine that had a chance to grow has been eaten by this wretched little worm—and that just isn't fair!

God asks him, " 'Do you have a right to be angry about the vine?' " And Jonah replies " 'I am angry enough to die' " (v. 9). Jonah's anger had festered. As it grew, he became more and more bitter. Then God really speaks to him, "Listen, Jonah, I provided shelter for you and you don't want me to provide shelter for these people. You are all upset about a vine, but you have no interest whatsoever in the city."

Have you ever noticed that sometimes God's people can be very bitter? Sometimes they get themselves all worked up about plants and animals, ecology and the environment, but show no concern for people. God's people can become deeply concerned about economics and politics—but they could not care less about a perishing world! How often God's kindness and compassion and concern are shown in sharp relief against the things that are a vital concern to his people.

In Jonah's prophecy, the emphasis is on the kindness of God. It is shown in his dealings with Jonah—and it is reflected in Jonah's initial response. It is shown in God's dealings with Nineveh, but most powerfully it is seen as it is contrasted with the attitude of Jonah.

Lessons to Be Learned

What are the lessons then that we can learn from the prophecy of Jonah?

1) God's kindness and his judgment are not incompatible. Both are clearly stated in this passage of Scripture.

2) God's resources are utilized for the fulfillment of his purposes. Surely that is one of the themes of the book. God provided all that would be needed to bring about his purposes.

3) God's kindness is to be reflected in his people. There must be no room for bitterness in God's people, unless we

allow God the right to be bitter. There can be no room for hardness of heart among God's people unless we permit God the privilege of having a hard heart, of treating us as we deserve.

God's kindness is to be reflected in his people—and God's kindness knows no limits. This was clearly exhibited in the facts of his grace, goodness, and kindness. Jesus descended into death for three days and three nights, as Jonah went down in the belly of the great fish. This was a sign: In the same way Jonah returned (from the dead, if you like) our Lord Jesus went into death and returned on our behalf. If we should ever doubt the kindness of God we must simply look at the cross. If ever we question the grace of God, we must look at Calvary. I wonder if we show the same lack of compassion and kindness to our world that Jonah did. We should ask the Lord to help us check our own attitudes—and examine our own hearts to see if there be any wicked way in us.

WHAT DOES THE LORD REQUIRE OF YOU?
Micah

MICAH IS THE SIXTH of the so-called minor prophets. The introduction to this book makes it clear that the prophet ministered during the reigns of three kings of Judah: Jotham, Ahaz, and Hezekiah, which makes him a contemporary of the prophets Hosea and Isaiah in the latter half of the eighth century B.C.

Micah's target audience was the people of both Judah and Israel. He lived in Moresheth, which was situated near Gath, about thirty miles southwest of Jerusalem. So the prophet apparently knew something of the corruption rampant in Judah's capital city—and he boldly spoke out in condemnation of what was going on. Also, he lived near the coastal road over which the traders traveled, so he was aware of the excessive traffic between Egypt and Jerusalem, and the resulting corruptive influence that had spread northeast from Egypt.

The Book of Micah divides neatly into three sections:

- Judgment pronounced on both Israel and Judah (chapters 1, 2)
- The restoration and reign of the Messiah (3–5)
- Divine punishment followed by divine mercy (6, 7)

Even though Micah was speaking primarily to his contemporaries, a timeless message for all ages comes down to us today. We can listen to what the Lord says through this ancient prophecy and go away challenged to answer the question, "What does the Lord require of you?"

The period covered by Micah's ministry is somewhat extensive, and his prophecy quite selective. It is a series of messages called oracles given at different times, in different circumstances, in all probability spanning a considerable length of time. It is important to recognize this if we are going to make any sense out of what Micah is saying. Second Kings 15–20 gives us the historical background of what was happening in Micah's day.

A Bit of History

God had brought the people of Israel out of Egypt, established them in the Promised Land, and eventually had given them a king. This is not what God wanted, but it is what the people wanted. Even though God told them that it would not work, they demanded a king anyway. Their first king, Saul, was a disaster. Then came King David who was a man after God's own heart, even though he was by no means perfect. After David came Solomon who reigned during the golden days of the monarchy in Israel. When Solomon died, however, considerable internal friction developed and the kingdom was divided in two, a northern kingdom called Israel, and a southern kingdom called Judah.

Two capital cities emerged, Samaria in the north, and Jerusalem in the south. These are the two cities to which Micah addressed his message. Micah predicted terrible devastation for Israel and Samaria: " 'I will make Samaria [Israel, the northern kingdom] a heap of rubble, a place for planting vineyards. I will pour her stones into the valley and lay bare her foundations. All her idols will be broken to pieces; all her temple gifts will be burned with fire; I will destroy all her images. Since she gathered her gifts from the wages of prostitutes, as the wages of prostitutes, they will again be used' " (1:6, 7). In other words, Micah is predicting the most dreadful destruction upon the northern kingdom of Israel.

What is happening to Israel is to be regarded as fair warning to Judah in the south. Here Micah uses very striking, dramatic words to describe how the judgment of God is going to come down upon them: "Because of this," he says, "I will weep and wail; I will go about barefoot and naked. I will howl like a jackal and moan like an owl. For her wound is incurable; it has come to Judah. It has reached the very gate of my people, even to Jerusalem itself" (vv. 8, 9).

Micah is referring to the Assyrian armies who have come upon Israel in mighty, irresistible force. What is taking place in Samaria, Micah says, will inevitably come to Israel. Without apology he points out that what is happening (historically and militarily) as the Assyrians encroach upon Samaria is directly related to the intervention of God in the affairs of men.

Micah had the same experience as the other prophets who came before him, and those who followed him. The people did not want to hear what he had to say. People rarely want to be told of judgment; they seldom want to be warned of what is happening. They prefer not that someone interprets the events unfolding on an international scale and show that God is intervening in men's affairs. Note this as well: Often those who can predict, prophesy, and interpret, who would bring a message from the Lord, find that it is like pulling teeth to get people to listen to the warnings. Accordingly, Micah finds it necessary to use a dramatic means of conveying his message. He goes around Jerusalem weeping and wailing, barefoot and partially clothed. He howls like a jackal and moans like an owl. It must have been exciting to have Micah around!

I had a very good friend in a Third World country, a Rhodes scholar, an absolutely brilliant man. He was the pastor of the largest church of his denomination. I remember he once debated a leading political figure on national television on the issue of legalized lotteries and gambling. He totally routed him. It was a national humiliation for that dignitary. My young pastor friend was particularly concerned that the people of his homeland were not listening to the Word of the Lord. As long as he told them what they wanted to hear it was great. As long as he preached that all was good and bright, that they would be prosperous and peaceful, that was super. But the young pastor was convinced that things were bad in his country and something needed to be done about it. People needed to be brought to repentance and to take God seriously.

He felt as if he had been hammering his head against a brick wall. So one day he came into church late for the Sunday morning service, to get the people's attention. He came in the back door instead of the front. That also aroused their attention. Instead of wearing his pulpit gown, he dressed himself in sackcloth and covered himself with ashes. Instead of carrying a Bible he carried a bell. He came in ringing his bell, and dressed in sackcloth and ashes. As a result, they fired him as their pastor and put him in a home for the mentally unstable. One day I talked to him and asked, "Did you have a nervous breakdown?"

"No," he said. "They decided that was what I had, but in actual fact I was trying hard to get their attention. I got it," he went on, "and when they gave me their full attention, they locked me up. They didn't want to know."

Such has always been the lot of the prophet. The person who tells people what is really happening in the world is not always welcome. Indeed, as Jesus said, "A prophet is not without honor, but in his own country. . . ." When a prophet comes with a hard message, he is bound to be unpopular. A prophet is one who warns of God's impending wrath. If people refuse to heed the message, if they refuse to repent, if they remain complacent, then the judgment eventually will fall.

This is the context in which Micah was ministering. God's message was a reaction to what Israel and Judah had been doing. What the Assyrians were doing was allowed by God because of Judah's transgression, and the sins of the house of Israel. God is talking directly to his people. Through Micah he is relating what is happening in the nation to the sins of the people of God.

A Dramatic Message

Micah cries: "Tell it not in Gath; weep not at all. In Beth Ophrah roll in the dust. Pass on in nakedness and shame, you who live in Shaphir. Those who live in Zaanan will not come out. . . . You who live in Lachish, harness the team to the chariot. . . . The town of Aczib will prove deceptive to the kings of Israel" (1:10, 11).

This latter part of the first chapter reveals the prophet's skill as a communicator. He uses a play on words, showing that he is as clever a punster as he is a strikingly gifted poet! For instance, Gath sounds like the Hebrew word for "tell." It is as if Micah were saying, "Tell it not in Tell City."

Ophrah means "dustiness" or "dust town," so he is saying, "In Dust Town you had better roll in the dust." Shaphir means "pleasant." "Pass on in nakedness and shame, you who live in Pleasantville," says the prophet. Zaanan sounds like the Hebrew word for "go out." Thus, Micah is saying, "Those who live in Go Out City never will come out again." Lachish sounds like the Hebrew word for "team," so his message is "Harness Town needs to harness the chariots and get out of here." Imagine an American preacher saying, "Living in Pittsburgh is the pits," or "Los Angeles is no city of angels," or "Wisconsin should only be pronounced Wiscon-*sin!*" That would get the people's attention.

Micah was having a problem getting his message across to the people so he chose this dramatic vehicle to reach them. But notice: All of the cities he mentions in his skillful poem are the ones that were being rolled under by the Assyrian steamroller. He is saying to the people of Jerusalem, "You know what happened to Gath, you know what happened to Ophrah, you know what is happening in Shaphir and Zaanan. Listen to what I am telling you! It is coming your way. It is really going to happen." Thus, in a very dramatic way he tries to get his message across.

In verse 16 he addresses Jerusalem and says, "Shave your heads in mourning for the children in whom you delight; make yourselves as bald as the vulture, for they will go from you into exile." That is straightforward enough, isn't it? He is saying to Jerusalem, "The exile is coming." He is saying to the people in Judah, "Because of your sin, because of your hardness of heart, because of the way that you are refusing to be God's people, take warning. What you see happening all around you is coming your way and it is only a matter of time."

Israel: Stewards of God's Property

In chapter 2 Micah moves into more specific detail as to what is upsetting God—and why it is necessary for God to intervene in such a way. In verses 1–3, he is telling the people of God that they have made their plans, but what they have overlooked is that God is making his plans too: "Woe to those who plan iniquity, to those who plot evil on their beds! At morning's light they carry it out because it is in their power to do it. They covet fields and seize them, and houses, and take them. They defraud a man of his home, a fellowman of his inheritance. Therefore, the Lord says: 'I am planning disaster against this people, from which you cannot save yourselves.'"

The specific matter that God is concerned about here needs a brief explanation. When the children of Israel came into the Promised Land, God ordained how that piece of real estate should be divided up among the tribes. Large parcels were then divided among families so that these clans or families would each have their own little piece of acreage. It was a very special covenant between God and them. The economic principles of ancient Israel were very different from the capitalistic or communistic systems of our day. The capitalist says, "Property belongs to me." The Communist says, "Property belongs to the state." But in Israel's economy, property belonged to the Lord. The people were simply stewards of it. That is why I find myself considerably more sympathetic toward the Old Testament system of economics than either the communistic or capitalistic system. We Christians need to bear these definitions in mind.

The Old Testament teaches us that the people of Israel had their little piece of land as stewards. It wasn't theirs; it was God's. And because it was God's, it was very wrong for people to abuse or covet the property of others. If you tried to buy other people's property, you took away their divine inheritance. You took from them something God had given them as stewards.

Obviously, from a practical and economic point of view, some of the people would do better with property than others. For that reason, some would amass a fortune and others would lose theirs. So, in order that things might be sorted out, every fiftieth year (Jubilee) property had to revert to its original owner. If anyone, because of unfortunate circumstances, had lost his property, other members of the family could redeem it for him. It had to be kept in the family and in trust. It wasn't the state's property, and it wasn't the individual's property—it was the Lord's. The people considered themselves as stewards of the land.

Two Problems

What was happening in Judah and Jerusalem during Micah's time? Entrepreneurs were working up great schemes to buy all the property. "How can we get all these peasants off the land?" they were saying. "How can we make sure that those who have very little end up with even less? How can we be assured that those of us who have much finish out with much more?" And God says, "Your attitude is utterly abhorrent to me. First of all, it shows a lack of social concern. Second, it demonstrates a singular lack of understanding of the whole principle of stewardship. That is totally unacceptable."

While the big businessmen were planning to buy up all the property of the peasants in the land where Micah lived, God is planning to visit them with disaster. "You will not, under any circumstances," he is saying, "go against my principles with impunity. Under no circumstances will you be able to override what I have said."

Judgment was bound to come. While the land-grabbers were making their plans, God was making his plans. This message applies to God's people today as well. We should always bear in mind that if we make our plans contrary to his plans, we are in trouble.

Notice another matter God is concerned about—false prophets. Micah observes, " 'Do not prophesy,' their prophets say. 'Do not prophesy about these things; disgrace will not overtake us.' Should it be said, O house of Jacob: 'Is the Spirit of the Lord angry? Does he do such things? Do not my words do good to him whose ways are upright?' " God asks (2:6, 7).

It appears that those who are going against God's rules regarding the management of property have their own little group of prophets who are encouraging them in what they are doing. "It is unthinkable to suggest that the covenant God will ever bring judgment on his people," they are saying. "We cannot tolerate this sort of thing at all. Therefore, let's get rid of Micah. He is a false prophet."

But while their prophets are saying one thing, God's prophet is saying another. This is the message of God's prophet. Notice the contrast. The false prophets and profiteers are saying: "Don't worry, guys. Everything is going to be fine. No judgment will come. We are doing things properly." On the other hand, God's prophet is saying, "You are dead wrong. You profess to be part of the covenant people, you profess that God is your covenant God, and you profess to be living your lives according to his orders—but you are not." When creed and conduct are in conflict, condemnation is inevitable.

In verse 10 of chapter 2, the prophet says, " 'Get up, go away! For this is not your resting place, because it is defiled, it is ruined, beyond all remedy.' " The "resting place" is the Promised Land. In a sarcastic summation of the other prophets, Micah says, " 'If a liar and deceiver comes and says, "I will prophesy for you plenty of wine and beer," he would be just the prophet for these people!' " (v. 11). In a scathing denunciation Micah declares that the profiteers have their prophets who will tell them exactly what they want to hear. What they tell them is far removed from what God has to say, but it is the kind of jargon that those people want to hear—and the kind of ministry they deserve. The contrast here is dramatic and striking: the profiteers have made their plans—God is making his plans. Their prophets say one thing, God's prophet says another. Their creed states one thing, their conduct contradicts it. "As a result of this," Micah says, "God is going to punish you. He is going to allow Jerusalem and Samaria to be taken into exile."

Micah wouldn't have won any popularity contests preaching this kind of message. But what a powerful message he brings as he lets the people know what is going to happen—and then tells them why. He tells them these people have been professing much and performing little. "God has been observing the contradiction between creed and conduct," the prophet says, "and he will not tolerate it anymore. Even though people using God's name are telling you what you want to hear," Micah says, "the real truth of the matter is quite different."

A Ray of Hope

Now the message takes a sudden turn. A ray of hope appears and that little ray of hope is the way God always operates. " 'I will surely gather all of you, O Jacob; I will surely bring together the remnant of Israel. I will bring them together like sheep in a pen, like a flock in its pasture; the place will throng with people. One who breaks open the way will go up before them; they will break through the gate and go out. Their king will pass through before them, the Lord at their head' " (vv. 12, 13).

What a brief but striking oracle this is in the midst of all the gloom and doom. Amidst the dire predictions and prognostications, a message of hope appears. The story is told in 2 Kings 19.

When the Assyrian king, Sennacherib, came and surrounded Jerusalem, the people flocked from the surrounding areas into Jerusalem. The king and his forces could not overcome Jerusalem. In the biblical record it is obvious that God clearly intervened in the situation. He overthrew the enemy, the Assyrians, and allowed the people who were bottled up in Jerusalem "like sheep in a pen, like a flock in its pasture," to escape. The place was thronged with people and eventually the gates of the city were opened to allow them to come out free. This is a dramatic fulfillment of Micah's prophecy.

This does not mean, however, that God failed to visit upon Jerusalem and Judah what he promised. Instead, it means that as people respond to him, he will always withhold judgment. As people are open to him, he will always be patient and long-suffering, bringing them to repentance. But people should never presume upon his patience. When the immediate danger of the Assyrians under Sennacherib was removed, all the dire predictions concerning the fall of Jerusalem and Judah did not come to pass. There was a measure of revival, a response to what God said. People did repent under Hezekiah, and dramatic things happened, but ultimately the people went back into their old way and Jerusalem and Judah finally fell, not under the Assyrians but under the Babylonians.

A Rebuke for the Leaders

In chapter 3, Micah goes back to deal with more of the problems confronting the people. In the first four verses he rebukes the leaders and rulers. Then in the second section or oracle, in verses 5–7, he states the case against the prophets—a dramatic contrast to what the prophets have been saying. He gives a personal testimony: "But as for me," he says, "I am filled with power, with the Spirit of the Lord, and with justice and might, to declare to Jacob his transgression, to Israel his sin" (v. 8). In the last oracle of chapter 3 he gives an exposé of the establishment at that time. It is summarized in these words: "Her leaders judge for a bribe, her priests teach for a price, and her prophets tell fortunes for money" (v. 11). In other words, the whole of the establishment is riddled with materialism and corruption.

What does the corrupt leadership do? Micah tells us: "Yet they lean upon the Lord and say, 'Is not the Lord among us? No disaster will come upon us.' Therefore because of you, Zion will be plowed like a field, Jerusalem will become a heap of rubble, the temple hill a mound overgrown with thickets." This prophecy was totally unthinkable and unacceptable to his hearers. But we find that eventually the people did listen to what Micah had to say, they did respond and Hezekiah the king was deeply impressed by Micah's message.

He led the people in repentance and there was a measure of blessing as can be seen in 2 Kings 19.

Look into the Future

In chapter 4 we see Micah looking off into the future. He has dealt with the immediate, but now he seems to be looking further ahead. He talks about future intervention by the Lord in the affairs of Israel: "In the last days the mountain of the Lord's temple will be established as chief among the mountains; it will be raised above the hills, and peoples will stream to it." Note how this dramatically contrasts with what he has been saying. He has just told them the mounds will be overgrown with thickets and Jerusalem will be a heap of rubble. Now he tells them that the mountain of the Lord's temple will be established. It will be chief among the mountains, raised above the hills; and instead of being deserted because the people have gone into exile the Israelites will stream to it.

What is he saying? That this very Jerusalem, instead of being overthrown—this temple, instead of being devastated—this Judah, that was held as a laughingstock because the judgment of God has come upon it, will be restored. There will be a dramatic and striking change among the people concerned. Not only is this change going to affect the people in Jerusalem and Judah; it is also going to affect all the nations of the world. Here Micah begins to deal with universal truth. He begins to speak of God's doing something through Jerusalem, through the holy place, that is going to have impact stretching to the uttermost parts of the earth.

The passage speaks for itself: "Many nations will come and say, 'Come, let us go up to the mountain of the Lord. . . .' " Jerusalem will be elevated to a place above all others. It will be the focal point of the world's attention. People will come and say, " 'Let us go up to the mountain of the Lord, to the house of the God of Jacob. He will teach us his ways, so that we may walk in his paths.' " The prophet goes on to describe the future: "The law will go out from Zion, the word of the Lord from Jerusalem. He will judge between many peoples and will settle disputes for strong nations far and wide. They will beat their swords into plowshares and their spears into pruning hooks. Nation will not take up sword against nation, nor will they train for war anymore. Every man will sit under his own vine and under his own fig tree, and no one will make them afraid, for the Lord Almighty has spoken" (vv. 2–4).

What is Micah saying here? He is saying that this very Jerusalem that was devastated, this very temple mount that had become the place of thickets, is going to become the focal point from which all the nations of the world will be blessed. From here will emanate the Word of the Lord. He will bring the standard of righteousness who will judge all people. There will come a time of universal peace when swords will be beaten into plowshares. The time is coming when men will have their own inheritance; terrorism will disappear. A man will be able to sit under his own fig tree and worship the Lord himself. No one will be able to make anyone afraid at that time.

How is this going to happen? By getting the right man in the White House? No. By straightening out the United Nations? No. By clearing up the economic situation? No. By making sure that we have adequate nuclear deterrents? No. How is it going to happen? The Lord Almighty has spoken and he is the one who in his own good time will bring things to order.

A Look Down the Centuries

In chapter 5, Micah records God's promise of a Messiah, the coming of the Christ of Christmas. As God's spokesman, Micah is looking right down the centuries. He sees what is happening immediately around him; he predicts what will happen in the immediate future; he calls the people to repentance; he tells them what will happen if they don't repent; and he reminds them that while they are making their plans, God is making *his* plans—and God's plans will prevail.

God's plans are centered in One who will come to Bethlehem Ephratah, whose origins are from of old. He will be mighty Jehovah's representative and he will ultimately rule over Israel. Micah is speaking of the King who shall come. This Messiah will come and he alone will prevail. He is the One who will be uplifted in Jerusalem. He is the One to whom the eyes of the nations will look. He is the One on whom universal attention will be focused.

When he reigns, justice will prevail. When he is in control, righteousness will be the norm. When he is supreme, weapons will be made into plowshares and people will live in peace. They will be no longer afraid.

What is Micah saying? The day is coming when God must be allowed to be God. Christ must be allowed to be Lord. The One whom God the Father has sent, his glorious Son, will become King of kings and Lord of lords. As far as God is concerned, that day is coming. This is our eschatological hope. This is what we as Christians, children of God, can look forward to.

But we can also apply it to our immediate situation. For when God is God of our lives, when Christ is Lord of our lives, no one can make us afraid. Justice will be what governs our heart and righteousness what we live for. From our very lives the Word of the Lord will go forth. "And he will be their peace," Micah says (5:5).

The Practical Requirements of the Lord

Micah has been speaking to his immediate contemporaries and now he asks the rhetorical question, "What does the Lord require of you?" (6:8) As with all good rhetorical questioners, he immediately gives the answer:

1. To act justly, not as the profiteers were doing in his immediate situation;
2. To love mercy, not as the establishment was doing in Jerusalem at that particular time;
3. To walk humbly with your God, not as the nation of Judah was doing.

What do these three things mean to me today—in light of what is happening on every hand, in light of the fact that God has spoken against sin and has told us that judgment will inevitably come?

He always warns in order that people might have time

to come to repentance. He has sent his Son to die, to rise again, and to ascend to the Father's right hand. This Son has promised to return again in glory. In light of all these facts, what does the Lord require of us now?

This is the crux of the matter and the answer is very simple and straightforward.

As far as my relationship to God is concerned, I am to walk humbly. Is that all he says? No, there's more. God requires me to walk through life humbly *with him*—day in, day out. I am to walk into the office humbly with my God. I am to move through my day-to-day affairs humbly with my God. This means I operate under his control in humble obedience to him. I am humbly repentant for that which grieves him. I am humbly dependent upon him at all times and for all things.

How will the world know that I am walking humbly with my God? They will know by the way I treat people. Those who walk humbly with their God have a passionate concern for justice being done in society, and a deep concern to treat people lovingly and mercifully. This is the message of Micah—the lesson God would have us learn as we read the words of this anything but "minor" prophet!

S e v e n
GOD IS GOOD AND ANGRY
Nahum

THE PROPHETS NAHUM and Jonah have something in common—both were channels of God's message to the city of Nineveh. Nahum, a contemporary of Zephaniah, Habakkuk, and Jeremiah, prophesied during the second half of the seventh century B.C., prior to the destruction of Nineveh in 612 B.C.

The Context of Nahum's Message

Jonah, you will recall, was God's messenger to Nineveh preaching a sermon of repentance to the city. The people heeded that message. As Jonah preached in the name of Jehovah, the people of that great, cruel city—the hated Assyrians—repented. And God delivered them from judgment. God had been wonderfully kind to Nineveh and to Jonah. God exhibited his kindness on every hand.

But a century and a half later, when Nahum preached,

the situation was different. Nahum came with another message for Nineveh. God was still dealing with the Assyrians,
but things were tightening up for Nineveh. God was now
responding to the fact that the Assyrians had "repented
of their repentance." Let me explain what I mean. To repent
is to change one's mind so thoroughly that it issues in a
change of direction. Under the ministry of Jonah, the people
of Nineveh changed their minds about God—and changed
their minds about themselves so thoroughly that they al-
tered the whole course of their lives. That's repentance.
Subsequently, however, they changed their minds about
their change of minds and went back to their old ways.
One of the worst things we can ever do is repent of our
repentance, as the ministry of Nahum clearly shows.

Now God sends Nahum to Jerusalem to speak about the
Assyrians. His message is powerful indeed. The city of Nineveh is to be totally wiped out. And that is exactly what
happened. The destruction of Nineveh was so complete
that in the centuries that followed armies marched over
its site without knowing that a city had existed there. And
Nineveh was no small village, as we pointed out in the
chapter on Jonah. The city walls have now been excavated,
and we have learned that they were approximately eight
miles in circumference. In addition to its massive walls,
Nineveh had a most remarkable canal and river system. A
center for all kinds of commerce, it was a city of monumental military might. Nineveh was a fearsome, awesome place.

The Assyrians who lived there were known for showing
no remorse whatsoever for their acts. When they attacked
their enemies they were so cruel that they would leave
cities utterly destroyed. They would carefully construct pyr-
amids of the skulls of the vanquished. Nineveh symbolized
an empire that struck fear into the hearts of everyone wher-
ever its armies went.

In the eighth century they surrounded the capital city
of Samaria and for three long years exerted phenomenal
pressure on Samaria. The most dreadful things happened

there. Finally, Samaria fell and Israel was overpowered, as the prophets Amos and Micah had predicted. And the people of Israel were taken away into captivity.

Later, Assyria turned its attention to Judah. The story is told in Second Kings 17–19. As the Assyrians moved into Judah, they overwhelmed all the cities until they came up against the last bastion—Jerusalem itself. There, Sennacherib, the king of the Assyrians, surrounded the city—but he was roundly defeated, not by Judah, but by a dramatic and dynamic intervention of God on behalf of his people. There the Assyrians suffered one of their rare defeats.

If this is the context in which God speaks about the people of Nineveh, and the Assyrians, through Nahum, obviously the people of Jerusalem were thoroughly thrilled over the circumstances. They have seen those who utterly terrified them overthrown. They have seen Israel taken into captivity. And they have known that their own days were numbered; survival, for them, was really questionable—but God has intervened. I imagine that in their joy, they forgot their basic problem. In this context Nahum speaks to them and reminds them that God is not through with the Assyrians yet. And he reminds them that the people of Judah also have something to answer for.

The Content of Nahum's Message

Now look at the *content* of Nahum's message. First of all, there is a message of consolation to the people of Jerusalem. The very name *Nahum* means "comforted" or "consolation" even though it's fairly difficult to find comfort and consolation in Nahum's word. After all, the Lord is a jealous and vengeful God, and he takes vengeance and is filled with wrath. Where is the comfort in that? What does it mean? What it means is this: Consolation is also very much a part of God's character. There is a message of consolation and comfort to the people of Jerusalem who have just escaped cruel punishment at the hands of the Assyrians. It is this: When you see your enemy coming in against you like a flood, always remember that if you do things God's way, the Spirit of the Lord shall lift up a standard against him (Isaiah 59:14, paraphrased).

This is a message of consolation that many of us need. We live in a world where evil apparently triumphs, where good people suffer. We live in a world where rascals get away with their crimes, where people who seem to tread underfoot with scorn and disregard the holy principles of God, seem able to do so with impunity. The wicked ones get away with evil, it seems, and the good ones suffer. The message of consolation to those who endeavor to do things God's way is this: *Don't ever think that the wicked will get away with it.* Don't think for a minute that we can tread underfoot divine principle and God's holiness with impunity. God is a God of justice and he is committed in the end to punishing wrong and rewarding right. That is Nahum's message of consolation to the people of Jerusalem. His message is a reminder of God's character.

God's Declaration of Purpose

Nahum also gives us a succinct statement concerning God's purposes: "Look, there on the mountains, the feet of one who brings good news, who proclaims peace! Celebrate your festivals, O Judah, and fulfill your vows. No more will the wicked invade you; they will be completely destroyed" (1:15). Similar words from Isaiah are often quoted—approvingly, of course,—by mission agencies around the world. They mean that the people who have suffered at the hands of the awesome Assyrians have already seen God intervene on their behalf. But they must understand something more. The day will come when the Assyrians will be utterly destroyed and Nineveh will be totally devastated. And the good news will come that Judah has been freed from its traditional enemies. This is God's purpose.

The message of consolation that comes to God's suffering people at all times is this: God is on the throne; he will ultimately triumph and evil will ultimately perish.

Some months ago I was talking to a Romanian pastor, exiled from Romania because of his stand against the government. He told me that the favorite book in the Bible, so far as the Romanian church is concerned, is the Book of Revelation. But he said it is not the favorite book of the church in Romania for the same reason that it is one of the favorite books of the church in America. He said that the church in America seems to be studying Revelation because it is sort of interesting—intriguing—the way things are going to work out. The American church is trying to make sure that it will never suffer. The church in Romania, on the other hand, is not interested in that aspect—because they are suffering and have suffered. He said they love the Book of Revelation because, first of all, it was written by John, the pastor of the church at Ephesus, after he had been sent into exile. The Romanian churches know what it is to have their pastors imprisoned and exiled.

Then he added this. Romanian Christians are suffering unjustly. They are being desperately abused and subjected to all manner of cruelty. Thus, the message of Revelation to them is the message of Nahum. It is this: God is God, and he is committed to seeing that good is ultimately rewarded. He is committed personally to seeing that evil will not finally triumph. Historians and archeologists, having examined the ruins of Nineveh and the artifacts of the Assyrians, substantiate this one point. What God said he would do through Nahum's prophecy he did.

A Message of Warning

Second, Nahum's warning to Nineveh is a reminder that God is a God of justice and grace. He always brings judgment upon evil; but before he does he always gives forewarning. He extends to the sinner the opportunity to repent. God receives no joy from seeing people remain unrepentant. That is why he gave Nineveh its warning. As Peter says, "[God] is patient with you, not wanting anyone to perish, but everyone to come to repentance" (2 Peter 3:9).

Notice in the warning, what God sees: "From you, O

Nineveh, has one come forth who plots evil against the Lord and who counsels wickedness" (1:11). This is a clear reference to King Sennacherib, who had come up against Jerusalem. He had lied concerning Jehovah, blaspheming the name of the Lord and bringing all kinds of evil upon the cities of Judah.

Also, Nahum tells us what God thinks about Nineveh. With dramatic clarity he simply says the most awful thing anyone could ever hear Jehovah say: " 'I am against you' " (2:13). Paul, writing to the Romans, said, "If God is for us, who can be against us?" What a message of consolation that is. But in Nahum we see the flip side: If God is against us, what does it matter who is for us? This is the overwhelming message of Jehovah to Nineveh. He has seen what has come out of Nineveh—he has formed his opinion about it—and this is what he thinks of Nineveh.

Some years ago, my friend Fred Train, an old missionary from Paraguay, was teaching at a Bible school in England. At the school there was a particularly obnoxious student who was so arrogant it oozed out of every pore. People avoided him; they just couldn't cope with him. They literally couldn't stand him. This student didn't care much for the ministry of missions. He didn't like to be told about people going out to reach the unreached.

One day he approached Fred Train and said, "I've just been on the phone to my father with regard to what you've been teaching. And my father says that he wants you to know that he thinks it would be the most dreadful waste of my life for me to go to the mission field. And he also wants you to know what he thinks about your message."

Old Fred Train, who was never one for backing up, looked at the student and said, "I'm very interested to know what your father thinks about you and me and my message and the Lord Jesus. But what interests me far more is—I wonder what the Lord Jesus thinks of your father."

I wonder what the Lord Jesus thought about Nineveh. I wonder what he thought about the Assyrians. I don't need to wonder long. God and his Son, sitting on the throne, say emphatically, unequivocally: "I am against you."

In addition, the message of Nahum to Nineveh is a reminder to Nineveh from God. Chapter 3 contains a clearcut historical reference. The kings of Assyria had gone right down all the way into Egypt. They had overthrown Babylon and occupied Israel; they had taken over Judah with the exception of Jerusalem. They were all-conquering. At one stage, they had overcome the Egyptian city of Thebes, which was very similar to their own city. But notice what Nahum says to them: "Are you better than Thebes, situated on the Nile, with water around her? The river was her defense, the waters her wall. Cush and Egypt were her boundless strength; Put and Libya were among her allies" (3:8, 9). Cush is Ethiopia. Put is Somalia.

"Yet she was taken captive and went into exile. Her infants were dashed to pieces at the head of every street. Lots were cast for her nobles, and all her great men were put in chains" (v. 10). Then he says, "You too will become drunk; you will go into hiding and seek refuge from the enemy."

Do you see the picture? God is simply saying to the Assyrians, "Listen, you know what you did to the city of Thebes. You know what confederacy backs them up. They had Ethiopia, Libya, and Somalia on their side—as well as Egypt. Everyone was ganging up against you, but you went in there and you overthrew Thebes. And the city of Thebes knew it was secure because of its fortresses, moats, and canals. You're exactly the same."

The point is this, if you could do that to Thebes, what can Jehovah do to you? And then Nahum goes on to say:

All your fortresses are like fig trees with their first ripe fruit;
  when they are shaken, the figs fall into the mouth of the eater.
Look at your troops—they are all women!

The gates of your land are wide open to your enemies;
   fire has consumed their bars.
Draw water for the siege, strengthen your defenses!
Work the clay, tread the mortar, repair the brickwork!
There the fire will devour you;
   the sword will cut you down and, like grasshoppers,
   consume you" (vv. 12–15).

Of course, this is exactly what happened. The enemies of Assyria, the Babylonians and the Medes, formed a confederacy and worked their way up toward Nineveh. At a critical moment, the Tigris River, on which the city was built, rose to flood level. So fast was the flood that it demolished the fortresses—the walls. And this is not only a biblical fact—it is historically confirmed as well. The whole city was destroyed. The day before, the people of Nineveh were enjoying a victory over those who were laying siege to their city. They had a party that night, an orgy. As they became drunk, the river flooded and the walls fell down flat. In the midst of their orgy, when the soldiers came in, their army was as defenseless as women. They were chewed right up. The city was completely overthrown and decimated. God had said this would happen—and it did.

Those who are skeptical about the minor prophets usually believe everything that the historians write. I'm not quite sure why. But what I've written here is historically verifiable. This is literally what happened to the city of Nineveh. The Assyrians were utterly and totally overthrown.

Instructions About Jehovah

As we have seen, the message of Nahum is, first of all, a message of consolation to Jerusalem, and secondly, a warning to Nineveh. But third, it's a message of instruction about Jehovah. The title of this chapter, "God Is Good and Angry," employs an expression we sometimes use. But I use it very carefully here. The first part of Nahum 1 describes God as an angry God. The second part speaks of him as being a good God. In the opinion of many, the two cancel each other out. They believe that to say God is good and also angry is to say contradictory things about him. Nothing could be further from the truth. God's great goodness and his awesome wrath and anger are inextricably bound up in each other.

Consider the awesomeness of Jehovah. Nahum says he is, without question, a jealous God. He is an avenging God, a God who displays wrath.

When the Bible says that God is jealous, we may have a problem understanding that. The word *jealous* is related to the word *zealous* which means to have a lot of zeal. To be jealous means to feel deeply about something—to be stirred emotionally and motivated into action because of that emotional involvement.

When we think of the zealousness (or jealousy) of God, we are thinking of a depth of emotion that stirs him into action. This depth of emotion is a zeal arising from his deep-felt love of his people and his deep-felt commitment to his own nature. If we can think in terms of God's being deeply moved, deeply committed—zealous for the object of his love and for the uniqueness and distinctiveness of his own nature and character—we will begin to understand what Scripture means when it says that the Lord is jealous. This speaks positively of his love, and the intensity of that love. It speaks positively of the activity of his love. So zealous is he in his love for his people, and in his own nature, he will brook no interference; he will let nothing get in his way. He is jealous of the object of his love.

When the Bible says that God is an avenging God, again we have a problem. When we think of vengeance, we usually think in terms of retaliation and we don't want to know about such a God. We think he would be a relic of primitive, Old Testament society; we much prefer the "New Testament God." That's how many people handle the problem, but it won't do, because the exact words that describe the "Old Testament God" also describe the "New Testament

God." In the New Testament, God is also described as being jealous, as exercising vengeance; the New Testament deals openly with his wrath. In fact, Jesus said more about these things than the Old Testament prophets ever did. The wrath of which the Old Testament prophets spoke was a temporal wrath. The judgment and vengeance and jealousy of which Jesus spoke, was an eternal one. So it is nonsense to try to set the Old Testament against the New. It can't be done.

Retribution, Not Retaliation

When the Bible says that God exercises vengeance, it does not mean that he is into retaliation. It means he is committed to *retribution*. Retaliation is merely "me getting even with you for what you did to me." Retribution speaks of a rigorous system of justice punishing you and me for what we have done. It's not a case of just getting even. Look at our prison system. We debate and argue over what is going on in that area. The philosophy used to be: "We're going to punish these people. We're going to use them as examples. They are the scum of the earth, so we'll throw them in these terrible places and keep them there. That's what they deserve. We'll show them our hatred and our punishment."

Fortunately, some enlightened people came along who instituted and initiated prison *reform*. Now the pendulum seems to have swung so far to the left that we've forgotten the idea of punishment in our concern with *reformation*. The system is saying: "Now listen, don't punish the criminal; just reform him; and if you need to punish him, do it as a means of deterrence." This is inadequate.

It is equally inadequate to be so concerned with reformation and deterrence that we overlook retribution. Why? If we don't punish someone for what he has done, we have insulted him, because we don't hold him accountable. If we don't hold him accountable, we are saying to him, "Because your actions were not significant we do not attach any significance to you." If we do punish people for what they have done, we're saying to them, "You did it. You're responsible. It was your action, and your actions are significant because you are significant."

Therefore, when we hear of God exercising vengeance, we hear him saying, "You are significant. You Assyrians are responsible. And to show you how significant you are, I personally will deal with you. I will punish you justly for what you did and I will punish you justly for what you are."

When we think in terms of divine vengeance, we're admitting that God places human beings in a position of tremendous significance. What he is saying is this: "Everything you do is significant—and when you do evil, you will be punished." God is certainly interested in deterrence; he is definitely concerned with protecting society. He is firmly committed to repentance and reformation. But don't ever make the mistake of thinking that God has gone soft as have so many of our judges. Nor should we make the mistake of thinking that God is like a medieval inquisitor who is so harsh that he never gives the sinner time to repent.

Zealous and Jealous

The awesomeness of our God is seen in the fact that he is zealous for those he loves; he is jealous for his own holy nature; and he will bring just retribution upon those who do evil.

Scholars tells us that almost every Hebrew word related to judgment and wrath is found in the first few verses of Nahum. They also tell us, incidentally, the Book of Nahum contains some of the most magnificent poetry ever written.

God's wrath is closely aligned to his holiness and righteousness. Here again, we encounter a problem. We don't like jealous people. Neither do we like people who retaliate, or those who lose their cool and turn upon us. Accordingly, we tend to dismiss what the Bible teaches about God. We have seen him merely as jealous and vengeful and losing his temper.

That is not what Nahum is saying about God at all. What the prophet is saying about God is this: His wrath is evidence of his righteousness, and his anger against evil is evidence of his stand for what is good. How do I know that a person stands for what is good? One of the best ways is to see how angry he becomes about the opposite of good—evil. We live in a very tolerant society today. In many ways it is good to see this tolerance. But it is a pernicious thing in other ways. We are not to be so tolerant that we will put up with anything. That is spinelessness. We need to be courageous enough to stand up for the right in the face of wrong. Do we want God to reward righteousness? Do we want him to make good ultimately triumph? Then we have no alternative but to accept a God of judgment and anger—holy, righteous, and pure. He must visit his wrath and his anger on all who depart from him and all who insult his moral character.

This is the message of Jehovah: God is angry, but we should see more than just his anger. I used to shiver when I saw a bumper sticker reading, "Jesus is coming again—and boy is he mad!" Still, I think that is a healthy balance.

We talk glibly about Jesus coming again. The New Testament tells us that when Jesus comes again, he will visit on his enemies fiery indignation and vengeance. We need to be sure we are taking God seriously!

A God of Patience

Finally, Nahum tells us that God exercises patience. He is jealous and vengeful, yes. He is filled with wrath. But he is ". . . slow to anger" (1:3). We see this repeatedly in both the Old and New Testaments. What does it mean? God is willing to give people the opportunity to face up to their evil, to see the wrong in their ways. He wants them to see the rightness of his righteousness and the inevitability of his judgment. God gives us time to repent. That is why he is slow to anger. There is no other reason why he would include this brief message of hope in the midst of his horrible indictment of Nineveh and the Assyrians.

Our legal and judicial systems have led to many miscarriages of justice, I'm sure. Innocent people have probably been executed. Others have been unfairly imprisoned (the Webb/Dotson case in Chicago in 1985 illustrates that aspect of the problem). The flip side of this is that many guilty people have escaped justice.

We have all offended God's moral righteousness. We have bitterly spat upon his holiness and ignored his principles. We have not done it with impunity, however. Be assured, God accepts full, personal, eternal responsibility for final judgment.

But that is only half the message, because "the Lord is good." How can I say God is good when I have just said he is a God of justice? His goodness is demonstrated by his jealousy, vengeance, wrath, patience—his commitment to ultimate justice. If God were not angry, he could not be good. If God did not commit himself to ultimate justice, he would not be just. If God did not commit himself to the final punishment of evildoers, he would not be righteous. It is only as I understand the sinfulness of my sins and the awesomeness of God's judgment that I really grasp the meaning of his grace and his goodness.

Do you know anyone who is not interested in grace? Do you know anyone who is not interested in mercy? Are there people who are not interested in God's goodness? They are the ones who refuse to believe that God is just, angry, righteous, and holy. Do you know what they believe? Deep down, they honestly believe they can live their lives without having to answer for their actions. The goodness of God offers us a refuge in time of trouble. The goodness of God promises to care for those who trust him. Those who are repentant, who are prepared to turn from their sin, casting themselves on God's mercy and goodness, will be recipients of his goodness. Basically, this is Nahum's message.

A Bridge Between the Old and New Testaments

What are the consequences of Nahum's message? To understand the answer to that question, we need to consider the message of the New Testament, particularly as outlined in Romans 2 and 3 where Paul extols God's righteousness and faithfulness. Paul speaks openly of human sin. And he goes on to explain forcibly about God's total commitment to judgment. He then develops the most wonderful theme of all: God, the awesome Judge, committed to holiness, righteousness, and justice, assumed our humanity. In the person of Christ he took our sin and our guilt. God, the Judge, became the Substitute and accepted our judgment. All our sin was heaped on him. The righteous, holy, unrelenting wrath of God was placed on Christ. Christ died, "the just for the unjust, that he might bring us to God. . . ."

Why did God deal with the Assyrians as he did? To show his righteous wrath against evil. To show that the most awesome, cruel regime imaginable was no match for the omnipotent God. To show categorically that evil in any form would ultimately be dealt with by a holy, righteous God. Why did he assume our punishment and in Christ die for us? He wanted us to recognize our own evil. He wanted us to realize how we break his laws and abuse his holiness. He wanted us to go free.

Paul in Romans tells us that the goodness of God leads us to repentance. Have you ever repented? Have you ever heeded the word of Scripture to flee from the wrath to come? Have you faced the fact that if you were to stand before a righteous God to answer for your life, you wouldn't have a leg to stand on? It is my prayer that this examination and exposition of the Prophet Nahum will help you see the love of God in action—and accept that love as your own.

Eight
GOD'S WAYS ARE NOT OUR WAYS
Habakkuk

"GOD'S WAYS ARE NOT OUR WAYS." We often use this expression without thinking about its meaning. Sometimes we say it out of frustration, sometimes out of confusion. At other times, we're simply expressing our feeling that the whole world in general (and our little part of it in particular) is in a mess. We have a hard time seeing how God fits into it (or more accurately, how our mess fits into our understanding of God).

Habakkuk is a lovely illustration of a man living in the midst of tumultuous circumstances. He was deeply concerned with the international situation of his day. Apparently it was hopelessly out of control. He wondered which way to turn. The tragedy, as far as he was concerned, was that in all the tumult going on, God didn't seem to be working. God wasn't making his presence felt, the prophet thought, and Habakkuk freely expresses his concerns, his frustrations, his doubts to God. As he does so, the modern reader gets a message loud and clear: God's ways are not our ways; he has entirely different ways of working than we do.

Habakkuk's Distress

The first two chapters of Habakkuk are a dialogue between Habakkuk and God. The third is a prayer.

The first thing we notice is the prophet's distress which he relates to God: "How long, O Lord, must I call for help, but you do not listen? Or cry out to you, 'Violence!' But you do not save?" (1:2). The tragedy confronting Habakkuk is something that disturbs many of God's people—and has done so through the years. It is why is evil and suffering rampant in our world? Goodness and justice, on the other hand, seem to fail. We believe in a God of justice and goodness. But we ask ourselves, if God is good and just, why does evil win out? Why do the good people suffer?

Some people never concern themselves about these questions. They never look further than their own lives. And if they are relatively successful and comfortable, they never ask the philosophical questions. They are never troubled by the theological questions. Morality is basically related to their economics and, provided they are in reasonable shape, such people get along just fine.

On the other hand, others are deeply concerned about who God is. They wonder how he relates to the world they observe around them. As they see evil apparently triumph, as they contemplate the suffering around them, they experience deep distress. Let me say this: Any Christian who is worth his salt will have some degree of distress of soul. He or she will be constantly dealing with the issue of who God is in the light of what is going on in his world. If we are not struggling with this, either we are not taking God seriously or we are not really taking a long, hard look at the world in which we live.

As a result of the distress the prophet relates, you will

notice that he expresses specific doubt: "Why do you make me look at injustice? Why do you tolerate wrong?" he cries (v. 3). Then Habakkuk goes on to enumerate the things that concern him.

It seems as if the heavens are brass and that his prayers are simply bouncing back. He hears them reverberating around the universe. In effect he says, "Why, God? How long must I call for help and you won't listen? It just seems that all I get back from you is a loud, stony silence."

He goes on, "Oh, there is another thing, God. I have been checking on the history of my people and I see you intervening down through the years. If we ever needed intervention it is now—and you don't intervene, God. Why is it that you are looking on injustice and you make me look on injustice, and you never rectify the situation? How is it, God, that you are so against wrong but you go on tolerating wrong? We are asking you to do something, God, but you don't."

The interesting thing about Habakkuk's doubt, however, is that it is freely expressed—but notice to whom he expresses it. Our world is full of people who are full of doubts about God, theology, and morality, but they never express those doubts to God. They form societies. They get gripe groups together or they pull out of the situation where they may possibly find some answers and isolate themselves in their bitterness. The important thing to notice about Habakkuk is this: While he is a man who has doubts and dares to express them, he doesn't make the mistake of ruling God out of the picture. That is the worst mistake one can make.

You and I are going to have doubts about God unless we don't think. We are going to have questions about God in the world unless, of course, we have opted to step out of the world. But the big thing is to be careful how we handle the questions and watch how we express the doubts. If I bring the doubts and the questions to God and seek his face about them, I will come up with an answer of some kind. But if I turn from him, if I isolate myself, if I throw the Scriptures away, if I reject the church and its people, then I'm in trouble. These are the reactions I hear constantly from those who don't handle doubts properly. Habakkuk is deeply distressed. But even though he is full of doubt he brings his distress and his doubts about God to God himself. That is the first part of the dialogue.

God's Answer

God has an answer: " 'Look at the nations and watch—' " he tells Habakkuk, " 'and be utterly amazed. For I am going to do something in your days that you would not believe, even if you were told' " (v. 5). In effect, God is giving Habakkuk a little preamble here. "All right," he says, "you're asking me for answers to prayer. Sit back, listen up—you are going to get one. What I'm going to tell you, you are going to find utterly unbelievable, you're going to find what I have decided to do totally incomprehensible."

" 'I am raising up the Babylonians, that ruthless and impetuous people. . . .' " (v. 6). God then goes on to describe the Babylonians. They are " 'fiercer than wolves at dusk. Their cavalry gallops headlong; their horsemen come from afar. They fly like a vulture swooping to devour; they all come bent on violence. . . . They deride kings and scoff at rulers. They laugh at all fortified cities . . . and capture them' " (vv. 7–10).

God is saying, "I'm going to work out something good from what is intrinsically bad. I'm going to bring justice through those who are unjust. I'm going to punish my people by using a people who are even worse than they. I have decided it. It is irrevocable."

This is why I have chosen to title this chapter "God's Ways Are Not Our Ways." If we are going to try to do something good, do we think of an evil means of doing it? If we are going to try to do something just, do we look for unjust people to bring justice about? No, we say, if we want justice we need just people, and if we want good to triumph, we need good people.

As far as God is concerned he chooses to act as he will, and this is the crux of the Book of Habakkuk. God has been warning his people Judah that judgment is coming. They have not heeded the warnings. They have had a roller-coaster experience of good kings, bad kings—and then good kings again. They have seen revival when they have done things properly—and then they have promptly turned away and gone back to their old ways. They have seen the dreaded Assyrians decimate Israel and Samaria. They have themselves been overthrown by the Egyptians. Egypt had attempted a takeover from the south. Under Josiah, Judah decided to try to cut off the Egyptians. The two nations met at Megiddo on the plains of Armageddon—and there Judah was soundly defeated. And the Egyptians were defeated by the Babylonians. All this happened during Habakkuk's time.

The dreaded Babylonians are emerging at the top of the pile of nations. King Josiah has been killed and Judah is in dire difficulty. In the face of this, Habakkuk is asking, "God, why don't you do something?"

And God answers, in effect, "I am, I am. Do you think the Assyrians were overthrown by chance? Do you think that Josiah and Judah were overthrown by coincidence? Do you think that the Egyptians were defeated by chance? Do you think that these people coming in from the east and from the south and from the north, converging in this particular place—that it is all by chance? You mustn't think that, Habakkuk. I am the Lord. I am the One who is sovereignly in control. I am going to work out my purposes. Habakkuk, go to the people one more time and tell them, my purposes for Judah are righteous. The Babylonians are on top of the heap, and those rascals are going to be the instrument of my judgment on Judah."

The Second Complaint

This sets the stage for Habakkuk's second complaint. The prophet is dismayed to hear God's answer, and now he asks: "O Lord, are you not from everlasting? My God, my

Holy One, we will not die. O Lord, you have appointed them to execute judgment; O Rock, you have ordained them to punish. Your eyes are too pure to look on evil; you cannot tolerate wrong. Why then do you tolerate the treacherous? Why are you silent while the wicked swallow up those more righteous than themselves?" (vv. 12, 13).

Habakkuk continues to ask, "Why?"

He is not raising any question as to God's existence. Nor is he stating any doubts about God's holiness. "My God, my Holy One," he says. Neither is he expressing any argument about God's judgment: "O Rock, you have ordained them to punish." There is no confusion about God's righteousness either: "Your eyes are too pure to look on evil; you cannot tolerate wrong."

Some people today doubt God's existence. They don't even give a thought to God's holiness. Many question God's judgment (they say it won't happen). Others have a hard time with God's righteousness because things are not working out the way they think they should. Instead of questioning themselves, they question God.

None of these questions enters Habakkuk's mind. His question is rather: "God, is what you are doing fair? Is this honestly the moral, ethical thing to do?"

I have come across many people who have decided to pull the plug on God. They haven't liked the way he worked; they haven't liked the circumstances of life. For instance, I have met single young people who have told me, "I used to be into Jesus and your church, but not anymore." When I check into what happened I find they became involved in our singles' ministry, but their primary objective was to find a mate. They expected God to give them a real neat partner. That sounds reasonable to me, for I have one myself. Why shouldn't everybody else have one?

These young people went to our singles' meetings, but they found this or that wrong with them. What they really found wrong was that the partner they thought God owed

them didn't show up. They saw other people getting part-
ners, but not themselves. They became disgruntled and discouraged (which is perfectly understandable), but the
tragedy is that they pulled the plug on God. They blamed
him. They didn't like his failure to do something about
their situation.

Other people do just fine in their spiritual life until they
get sick. Then for some reason they think they have the
inalienable right to constant good health. Instead of turning
to God in their extremity (allowing God to be God and
work things out his way), they turn against God.

We as Christians must take God seriously. He reserves
the right to be God, to work as he will. If we allow him
to work as he will, we may ask all kinds of questions. But
we must be very careful not to turn from him instead of
asking questions.

This is what Habakkuk says: "I will stand at my watch
and station myself on the ramparts; I will look to see what
he will say to me, and what answer I am to give to this
complaint" (2:1). In other words, Habakkuk makes a very
wise decision; he says, "I will wait on the Lord." That can
come across as a terribly pious platitude, even in the context
out of which Habakkuk was speaking. We are typically im-
patient. We want things to happen, we want solutions yes-
terday. We feel we have the right to an answer to every
question, a solution for every problem, and health for every
sickness. We should have been around with Habakkuk in
Jerusalem when the Babylonians were coming. His doubts,
his dismay, and distress were clear to see in the way he
acted and spoke. Habakkuk would have said, "I've got some
real questions about God, too. I don't like the way he is
doing things—and if he would let me organize it for him
we would certainly have done it a much better way. But
I will tell you what I am going to do: I am going to take
time, go to my tower, and wait on him. I am going to take
time to let him talk to me and get my thinking in line
with his."

Our big problem is that we want to get his thinking in line with *ours*. What Habakkuk is saying is this: "I'm going to take all the time necessary to get my thinking in line with God's." Then God, when he has Habakkuk on his tower of meditation, can begin to declare something to him.

A Quiet Place

Do you have a secret place, a quiet place where you can escape the hurly-burly of this fast-paced world? Do you have an area where you can take time to think and ponder and meditate?

People often ask me how I'm able to do all I do. They don't believe me when I tell them one of the reasons I am able to do all this is the travel schedule that I have. Why is that? Because I have a high tower (it is about thirty-six or thirty-eight thousand feet high!) in the back of an airplane. That is the time when I get away from the demands of the telephone and people. I have a chance to be alone with my books and to sit quietly in prayer. For hour after hour I have a chance to think and meditate and pray.

What happened when Habakkuk took time to meditate and pray? He tells us what the Lord said to him: " 'Write down the revelation and make it plain on tablets so that a herald may run with it' " (2:2). The translations of this verse differ, but what the Lord is saying in effect is this: "I have a declaration to make, and this declaration is not just for you, Habakkuk. It is a declaration that has to be widely broadcast. I want you to recognize that the outcome is absolutely certain. There will be a delay, but wait for it. When I am ready I will act and not a minute before."

God is always right on time. But we must patiently wait for him to act, " 'For the revelation awaits an appointed time . . . though it linger, wait for it; it will certainly come and will not delay' " (v. 3). Then Jehovah goes on to point out that the offenders are going to be the means of bringing judgment. He is not suggesting for a moment that because they are to be the instruments of bringing judgment on Judah that they themselves will not be judged. Rather, he says to Babylon, "I am going to deal with the Judeans and then I will deal with you as well. But I'm going to use you as an instrument first—then I will turn my attention to you."

God is going to deal with everyone in righteousness, holiness, and justice. This is the way he must work.

God says to Habakkuk: " 'See, he is puffed up; his desires are not upright . . . indeed, wine betrays him; he is arrogant and never at rest. Because he is as greedy as the grave and like death is never satisfied, he gathers to himself all the nations and takes captive all the peoples' " (see 2:4, 5).

The Righteous Remnant

Notice in particular a little phrase in the middle of verse 4: ". . . but the righteous will live by his faith. . . ." This phrase crops up later in the New Testament, and is a crisp, clear statement of a gigantic spiritual truth. In effect God is saying, "In absolute justice and righteousness, in absolute morality I am going to judge Judah and then I will judge the Babylonians.

"But in marked contrast to those people who are going to feel the judgment of God," he says, "there will be a righteous remnant of people in the midst of all this devastation. This righteous remnant will be characterized by one thing: their faithfulness."

Anyone familiar with the New Testament knows the expression, "the just shall live by faith," or "they will be justified by faith." In both the Hebrew and the Greek, *faith* and *faithfulness* come from the same root word. In their thought the ancient writers realized something that we have tended to overlook: If you have genuine faith, it will be exhibited by faithfulness. In other words, if I have faith in a faithful God, others will know it by the way that I live. The God in whom I claim to have faith will be so real to me that I will make him real to you.

God is saying to Habakkuk, "I am absolutely just and holy. I am absolutely in control, and I am going to work things out my way. My will is irrevocable. Nothing will change it. You can be certain of it. Those who deserve the justice of God will come under my judgment. But in the midst of judgment and devastation, there will always be a remnant who have faith in me. These exhibit their faith by living faithfully before me."

The history of Judah and Israel, the history of God's people and the Christian church reveals this: There has always been a remnant right down through the centuries which has exhibited trust and dependence on the living God. They have come before him humbly and in repentance. We know that they live and have lived by faith because of their faithful lives.

One of the tragedies of the church of Jesus Christ in the western world today is that we have made it so easy to "believe" that we have put a great chasm between coming to faith and living faithful lives. Accordingly, it is not uncommon to find people who make loud protests of faith in Jesus Christ. Nevertheless, they live in direct disobedience to Christ. Listen to what Habakkuk (and the New Testament) says about this: "Those who are not living by faith and showing it in their faithful lives come under the judgment of God. On the other hand, those who in the midst of the judgment are living by faith in him and showing it by their faithful lives, will be preserved."

I make this next point carefully. Some of you reading these words profess your faith in Christ—but you are actually unfaithful to him. I know you are unfaithful to God because you are not even faithful to your wives (or husbands). How can you claim faith in the living Christ, and being faithful to God, when you are living in unfaithfulness to your spouse? It cannot be done. The righteous shall live by his faithfulness! How can we profess to be new creatures, to be made alive in Christ, and show no evidence of this life? If we fail to do so, we cheapen, we disgrace the gospel.

The conclusion of the matter is given in verse 20: " '. . . the Lord is in his holy temple; let all the earth be silent before him.' " In our dialogue with God, this is where we begin and end.

In the beginning Habakkuk was all distressed, expressing his doubts. Then God responded and revealed his decision. That didn't help Habakkuk a bit. Instead it intensified the sheer dismay that he felt. What did he do then? He quietly waited on the Lord, and then the Lord made a powerful declaration about his own holiness and righteousness. He reminded the prophet that there will always be room in God's mercy for those who escape his judgment when by faith they come to him. Their repentance and trust in him, and their obedience, will reveal the reality of their faith.

That is the message of Habakkuk. There is a great mission call here. If we have received a message of the holiness and righteousness of God, and the justice and judgment of God, by the same token we've received the message of the forgiveness of God. We know people can come to God through faith in Christ and his shed blood. They can know forgiveness. That is the message we are to spread to the uttermost parts of the earth. We are to call men and women to faith that is exhibited by faithful lives. That is the declaration that God makes.

Habakkuk's Response

What is Habakkuk's response? Look now at the third chapter. First of all, he respectfully requests divine mercy: "Lord," he says, "I have heard of your fame; I stand in awe of your deeds, O Lord. Renew them in our day, in our time make them known; in wrath remember mercy" (3:2). Then Habakkuk proceeds to pray for his beleaguered people. The Babylonians are bearing down on them, tragedy is inevitable. Confronted with the whole situation, the prophet prays and pleads for divine mercy. Then he carefully recounts divine history. He remembers what God has done and how God has revealed himself. He has a clear idea of who God is and he patiently awaits divine activity: "I heard and my heart pounded, my lips quivered at the sound; decay crept into my bones, and my legs trembled. Yet I will wait patiently for the day of calamity to come on the nation invading us" (v. 16).

He is well aware of what the Babylonians can do. History is replete with their desperate, terrible exploits. But he says he will wait patiently for the day of calamity to come on them.

"Yes," Habakkuk prays, "I know that judgment is coming on us. But, Lord, I trust you in the midst of the whole thing. I trust you to act. I trust you to work out your purposes. I will trust you through thick and thin." Then he comes out with the most joyful affirmation of divine sovereignty one can possibly read anywhere: "Though the fig tree does not bud and there are no grapes on the vines, though the olive crop fails and the fields produce no food, though there are no sheep in the pen and no cattle in the stalls, yet I will rejoice in the Lord, I will be joyful in God my Savior. The Sovereign Lord is my strength; he makes my feet like the feet of a deer, he enables me to go on the heights" (3:17–19).

In modern language he would be saying: "Though my job goes and my health fails, and the forces of evil seem to have things their own way; and even though the economy doesn't work the way I want it to, and the election doesn't work out the way I hope, and I'm not appreciated among my friends, and everything goes wrong, I won't pull the plug on you, Lord. I won't resent you, Lord. I will have my doubts and questions about how you are working. I won't stop questioning—but there is one other thing that I won't stop doing either. I won't stop rejoicing in you. For you are my rock and you are my strength."

We can best summarize the message of Habakkuk by asking some questions. Do we doubt? Are we troubled by the silence of God? Do we doubt because of disappointments? Do problems confuse us? Somebody has said that, given the world we live in, if God is God he is not good— and if God is good he isn't God. That shows a very shallow understanding of who God is. But that is where many people are. They have doubts. One more question: If you have doubts, will you wait? Will you wait on God and trust in him? You should, because if you consider the alternatives they are too unspeakably horrible!

Some people have resolved their problems about God by the simple expedient of getting rid of him. In doing so they introduce the most horrendous problems and haven't solved a thing.

Waiting On God

Will you wait and let God speak to you? You are not going to understand him quickly and you are not going to come up with solutions overnight.

As you are waiting on God, are you being faithful? Are you full of faith? Are you trusting him where you can't see? Will you trust in him where you don't have all the answers? Will you still have that firm rock under your feet even though there are all kinds of doubts? Faith is the very basis of life. Try living without faith and you will discover you can't.

One day I got in a little plane to make the flight home to Elmbrook. The guy who was to fly the aircraft said it would take us two hours and ten minutes to get there. I believed him, and got into the plane. On the way home we were in the overcast all the way. We couldn't see a thing—we just trusted the instruments. Then a voice spoke to us on the radio, telling us to descend from 7,000 to 2,700 feet. The voice promised us we would come out of the overcast, and we did. The minute we came into the clear at 2,700 feet a runway appeared right in front of us. We trusted the voice, we trusted the instruments, I trusted the pilot, I trusted the plane.

That is how life operates. Do you ever trust God? The nice thing I liked about that pilot was that he said, "Let's pray," and the minute we touched down he said, "Now let's pray again." We committed ourselves to God and then we had the courtesy to thank him at the end.

Do you live by faith? Can I tell by your faithfulness that you are a person of faith? Are you rejoicing? Are you rejoicing in God by discovering more and more who he is and learning more and more to discount the circumstances that you have? If your lifestyle is governed by your circumstances, you may as well settle down to being pretty miserable, the older you get. But if your life is governed by your God, you may as well fasten your seatbelt, for you will find life increasingly exhilarating the older you get. The more you get to know God, the more exciting you will discover him to be.

All this can be wrapped up in one thought: God's ways are not our ways! Anyone who has determined that he or she wants to get God's mind in line with his, is in trouble. But if you are prepared to take the time necessary (and the faith and obedience) to align your thinking with his, however long it takes, get set for a glorious trip through life!

GOD'S TOUGH AND TENDER LOVE
Zephaniah

ZEPHANIAH WAS THE LAST of the minor prophets to write before the captivity. He gave warning of the approaching judgment—the coming time of wrath upon a disobedient Israel. God's tough but tender love is clearly demonstrated in this prophecy.

It is difficult for us as humans to balance the tough and tender aspects of love. I recently read about an eleven-year-old golfer—a tall, blond kid, big for his age. He was developing so quickly that he was able to compete with fifteen-year-olds and beat most of them. This young fellow could hit the ball a mile, they said. He had a superb swing and the style and poise of an adult. One day he made a bad shot and angrily threw his club as far as he could. His father, who was playing with him, walked over and picked up the club. He brought it back and handed it to the boy saying, "Here is your club. The next time you do that will be the last time you ever set foot on this golf course!"

Jack Nicklaus took the lesson to heart. Those who are interested in golf are probably glad that Jack's father didn't just say, "Naughty, naughty, you mustn't do that!" We're also glad he didn't bend a club over Jack's head and kick him off the golf course right then! There was a toughness about that father's love, but there was a tenderness also, because he knew his boy was only eleven.

Tough and tender love. A young fellow, busy stealing cars in California, was eventually caught and hauled before the judge. Wisely, the judge didn't just send him to jail. He knew that there the boy would be introduced to all the advantages of a jailhouse education. There was a high probability that this amateur car thief would become a professional. Yet, on the other hand, the judge knew that he couldn't just let the boy off. So he tried to blend some toughness with tenderness. He sent the young fellow to a ski camp and told him to stay there until he mastered the sport of downhill skiing. The boy had to fit into a grueling training program—but those who are interested in downhill skiing are glad that the judge dealt firmly with Bill Johnson. He became the gold medal winner in Alpine skiing at the 1984 Olympics. The judge wasn't so tough that he broke him—but he wasn't so tender that he let him get away with his crime lightly.

Tough and tender love is what is needed in our dealings with each other. When we think of God we remember that he is a God of love. When we think of his love, however, we must remember that God's love is of the tough and tender variety. Unfortunately, most of us think only of the tender side of God's love. We completely overlook the tough aspect of it. It's hard to understand that underlying the toughness is an infinite tenderness.

Good King Hezekiah

Zephaniah, this prophet of the tender and tough love of Jehovah, tells us he is "the son of Cushi, the son of

Gedaliah, the son of Amariah, the son of Hezekiah, during the reign of Josiah, son of Amon king of Judah." This is the only place in the minor prophets where we are given the whole heritage of the prophet. Probably one reason it is given is to take the reader back to Hezekiah. This helps us to see the context in which these events took place. You remember that Hezekiah was a godly king. While he didn't do everything absolutely right, he had a superb reign. He is a marvelous example of what a godly ruler should be.

The Bible has much to say about King Hezekiah: He ". . . trusted in the Lord. . . . There was no one like him among all the kings of Judah, either before him or after him. He held fast to the Lord and did not cease to follow him; he kept the command the Lord had given Moses. And the Lord was with him; he was successful in whatever he undertook. He rebelled against the king of Assyria and did not serve him. From watchtower to fortified city, he defeated the Philistines, as far as Gaza and its territory" (2 Kings 18:5–8). Here is a picture of a godly king, one who did things the way God wanted them done. King Hezekiah led his people properly.

It is interesting to contrast Hezekiah's godly leadership of Judah with what was happening in the neighboring state of Israel, which was being attacked by the Assyrians and eventually fell.

Zephaniah's Heritage

As things go well for the Assyrians and they overrun Israel, they decide that Judah is next on their list. But under Hezekiah's leadership, Sennacherib, king of the Assyrians, is defeated at the very gates of Jerusalem. We read: " 'Therefore this is what the Lord says concerning the king of Assyria: "He will not enter this city or shoot an arrow here. He will not come before it with shield or build a siege ramp against it. By the way that he came he will return; he will not enter this city," declares the Lord. 'I will defend this city and save it, for my sake and for the sake of David my servant' " (2 Kings 19:32–34).

This is Zephaniah's heritage as he remembers Hezekiah's rule, when people did things God's way. When Samaria and Israel were falling under the Assyrians, and had been led away into captivity, the Lord mightily defended Jerusalem and Judah against the attacker. The Assyrians were defeated as God intervened.

Manasseh's Evil Reign

Look at what happens, however. After Hezekiah died, his son Manasseh came to the throne and was Hezekiah's exact opposite. In Second Kings 21 we read, "But the people did not listen. Manasseh led them astray, so that they did more evil than the nations the Lord had destroyed before the Israelites" (v. 9).

The people had witnessed Hezekiah's godly rule and had seen God intervene on their behalf. They knew the right way to go. But as soon as Hezekiah died, they came under Manasseh's leadership. He rejected everything that his father Hezekiah had stood for and he returned to heathen practices. Even when he was warned by God's Word and the prophets, he would not listen. The remarkable thing is that the people would not listen either. They gladly turned to ways more evil than what had characterized them before when others were destroyed for their rebelliousness before their very eyes. This is a sad commentary on the remarkable fickleness of human beings.

Notice how God handled this situation: " 'I am going to bring such disaster on Jerusalem and Judah,' " God says, " 'that the ears of everyone who hears of it will tingle. I will stretch out over Jerusalem the measuring line used against Samaria and the plumb line used against the house of Ahab' " (2 Kings 21:12,13). In other words, God says, "I'm going to deal with Jerusalem and Judah in exactly the same way that I dealt with Samaria and Israel. They had their opportunity and blew it."

Then he uses another graphic metaphor: " 'I will wipe out Jerusalem as one wipes a dish, wiping it and turning it upside down. I will forsake the remnant of my inheritance and hand them over to their enemies' " (vv. 13,14).

This is the immediate background of Zephaniah's prophecy. The people had come through Hezekiah's rule, and had rejected what Hezekiah said. Then they had gone further astray under Manasseh. Now disaster looms before them, but, amazingly enough, God is still willing to give them another chance. After Manasseh dies, young Josiah comes to the throne. And as he does, we read some remarkable things about him.

Good King Josiah

Every young person ought to read about this king. As parents we should read the story of Josiah to our children. He was only eight when he came to the throne, and he reigned for thirty-one years. Some interesting things happened in the eighteenth year of his reign, the most important of which was the discovery of the Word. The Scriptures had been lost in Jerusalem until a scroll was rediscovered in a dusty corner of the temple. When the young king was told about this fabulous find he began to read it assiduously and insisted that it also be read to the people. As the Word of God was read, the people discovered what God was saying to them. " 'Great is the Lord's anger that burns against us because our fathers have not obeyed the words of this book,' " cried Josiah. " 'They have not acted in accordance with all that is written there concerning us' " (2 Kings 22:13).

During Josiah's reign Zephaniah prophesied and ministered. When the book of God was found, a dramatic change took place in Jerusalem. The people were overcome as they realized how far short of God's plan they had fallen. And they responded to Josiah's leadership: "He read in their hearing all the words of the Book of the Covenant, which had been found in the temple of the Lord. The king stood by the pillar and renewed the covenant in the presence of the Lord—to follow the Lord and keep his commands, regulations and decrees with all his heart and all his soul, thus confirming the words of the covenant written in this book. Then all the people pledged themselves to the covenant" (2 Kings 23:3, 4).

Revival came under Josiah's rule. Whereas under Manasseh, everything fell apart, under godly King Hezekiah everything went well. This is the biblical pattern; it happens over and over again. A good leader brings blessing; a bad leader brings bad times.

At what stage in Judah's up-and-down history did Zephaniah prophesy? If he prophesied before the book of the covenant was discovered, it is easy to understand what he is saying. If, on the other hand, he prophesied afterward, and after Judah was renewed, we might well agree with what many scholars have assumed—the revival was purely superficial; it was only cosmetic. We don't know the answer to that question, but it is something to keep in mind as we read Zephaniah.

Against this background Zephaniah begins to speak to the people. His theme particularly is God's love for his people. Isn't it amazing? The ungrateful people have been so fickle, they have vacillated, they have contradicted and disobeyed all that God told them. The more God deals with them in mercy and grace, the more calloused and superficial they become. God's love persists.

What a message this is for our generation. If ever there was a time when people have had ample evidence of the goodness and patience of God—if ever there has been demonstrated convincing proof of his grace—it is today. Yet how remarkable it is that people go their headstrong way. They respond when the heat is on, but as soon as things get better, they go back to their old ways.

Do you remember how people began to conserve oil when the shortage first hit a few years ago? We began to buy smaller cars, and we all became concerned that we had been squandering unrenewable resources. Then someone told us that there was a glut of oil and guess what happened? Big cars began selling again. Temperatures in office buildings went up, and we went back to our old ways. When human beings have to shape up, they do—and then, when stringent standards are relaxed, they go back to their old ways. Don't misunderstand me. I am not equating driving a big car with the sins of Samaria and Israel. Neither am I saying that God is going to deal with you and your big car in the same way he dealt with Samaria and Israel. Knowing how people can jump to the wrong conclusions, it is important that I emphasize this!

The Nature of God's Concern

In his tough love for his people, God is concerned about the people's attitude: "Woe to the city of oppressors, rebellious and defiled! She obeys no one, she accepts no correction. She does not trust in the Lord, she does not draw near to her God" (3:1, 2). The prophet is speaking of Jerusalem, and the people of Judah, God's chosen people who should remember their glorious history. They are people of the covenant who have been highly privileged to know God.

The prophet speaks of their rebellious attitude. They will not obey God or those to whom God has delegated his authority. Not only this; they also have closed minds. They refuse correction and reject advice. "Get off my back," they say in effect. "Who do you think you are, interfering in my affairs? I can do my own thing. I have as much right to my opinion as you have to yours."

The people were exhibiting a self-sufficient spirit. They felt no need to trust in the Lord, for they could handle their own affairs, thank you. As far as they were concerned, they weren't even interested in incorporating the Lord as their source of strength.

The final thing Zephaniah says about them is that they do not draw near to the Lord. In other words, they are not concerned to live a holy life. They do not desire to develop and practice the disciplines of a devotional attitude. Worship is not a top priority in their daily experiences. They never even think to "draw near to the Lord."

As a result of these things, the Lord says an unscrupulous society is being formed. The same characteristics are apparent on every hand in our world today. And God is just as concerned now as he was then.

God's Complaint

Consider the nature of the Lord's complaint against his people: " 'I will stretch out my hand against Judah and against all who live in Jerusalem. I will cut off from this place every remnant of Baal, the names of the pagan and the idolatrous priests—those who bow down on the housetops to worship the starry host, those who bow down and swear by the Lord and who also swear by Molech, those who turn back from following the Lord and neither seek the Lord nor inquire of him' " (1:4–6).

God is complaining about the fact that his people are engaging in all kinds of pagan practices. They have returned to Baal worship, they are including the names of the pagan gods in their worship experiences, and they are listening to and following the lead of priests who are engaging in all kinds of idolatrous behavior. They are continuing to maintain a godly attitude externally—but as far as their hearts are concerned, they are disobedient. They won't accept correction or trust the Lord. They are incorporating in their worship all kinds of pagan practices. Even though they bow down and swear by the Lord, making great vows and commitments and covenants to him, at the same time they are swearing by Molech (an obscene heathen god to whom the people actually sacrificed their infant children). The people of Jerusalem are now so far into pagan religion that they are incorporating what is totally abhorrent to God in their worship. Some of them have done this and still call it "Jehovah worship"; but others, who used to follow the Lord, have turned back to their former pagan ways.

We can "turn back" in a variety of ways. For example, sometimes I encounter people in the city where I live who ask me, "Stuart, remember me?"

I look at them and suddenly I do remember. They go on: "We used to go to your church." And I reply, "Oh sure, I remember you. You used to come to the old church. How are things with you and the Lord?"

"Oh," they reply, "we gave that up ten years ago." That is one way of no longer following the Lord. There is another way, and that is to go on externally following, wearing the mask of spirituality—but in reality walking in the opposite direction.

As a boy I remember hearing Campbell McAlpine, the preacher, affirm this: "God said of his people at one time that they turned their backs on him but not their faces." Such people continue looking in one direction, but they are all headed in the opposite direction. The Bible calls them "stiff-necked," for obvious reasons! Such people turn their backs on God but not their faces.

There are many, many ways of turning back from following the Lord. Some do it blatantly and openly. They come to a major point of decision in their lives and decide against God's will and way. They do it knowingly; it is a conscious, premeditated act. God categorizes such people right along with those who are engaging in all kinds of pagan worship.

There's another group of people against whom God complains: that great segment of society that is disinterested in God. These are the callously complacent. They say they can handle things their own way and they see absolutely no way to believe in God or to follow him—or to take him seriously at all.

It's probably true that the city of Milwaukee, in whose area our church is located, has almost as many churches as bars. Yet a majority of Milwaukee's population will not darken the doors of a church. In that good, solid, midwestern, conservative city there is a pervasive air of practical unbelief. Some may say they believe in God, but their hearts are far from him. This is the complaint that God had concerning Jerusalem—and I believe it is a valid complaint today.

God's Commitment

Notice something else. God has outlined his concern and complaint. Now he straightforwardly outlines his commitment: " 'The Lord within her [Jerusalem] is righteous; he does no wrong. Morning by morning he dispenses his justice, and every new day he does not fail, yet the unrighteous know no shame' " (3:5).

In other words, in the midst of a city and society like this, God is present, powerful, and righteous. He is just and totally committed to what is right. He is a beacon of righteousness in the midst of unrighteousness. He is a pillar of justice in the midst of injustice. He is the quiet voice of truth in the clamor of evil.

In my judgment there is no more powerful verse in Zephaniah than this: " 'Be silent before the Sovereign Lord, for the day of the Lord is near' " (1:7). In the midst of all the clamor and confusion, God calls his people to reality.

Throughout this book, and throughout the minor prophets, this is the recurring theme: The Lord is in the midst of a rebellious, unbelieving people. This righteous God is calling people to live rightly before him. This holy God can be counted on to deal justly and in utter holiness. That means that there will be a final evaluation. For that reason there definitely will be a judgment day.

The People's Reaction

What has been the reaction of the people? They seem to listen but then they go back to their wicked, rebellious ways. Another prophet and a new king come along, and the cycle is repeated. Then God puts the heat on them again in some situation, and they repent. But they soon go back to their old ways.

In the end God speaks through Zephaniah and calls the people together silently before God. That silence speaks volumes, because it means there are no more excuses and no more arguments. The complaints and debate have come to an end. God says in effect, "Yes, you be quiet and listen to me. I am God." Figuratively rolling up his sleeves, God says to Jerusalem, "This has gone too far. I am not going to put up with this any longer. If I allow you to persist in this behavior then my name will be totally destroyed and you will feel that you can get away with unrighteousness—and this cannot be!" This is the tough love of God speaking: " 'I will sweep away everything from the face of the earth. . . . I will stretch out my hand against Judah and against all who live in Jerusalem' " (1:2, 4).

Do you honestly, genuinely believe in the judgment of God? If I were to try to pinpoint the area of major unbelief in so-called "Christian America," I would emphasize this—we don't really believe in a holy righteous God. We don't believe in a God whose love is tough.

Personally, as a human and a preacher, I don't know how to get people to become silent before God. If I knew how to do it, I would. Incidentally, it doesn't worry me too much because I have never met any preacher who could do it. This is something only the Spirit of God can do—taking the Word of God and impressing it on individual hearts. Faced with the facts, they must decide whether to believe or not. Thus they respond to God's tough love.

Note this, however. At the same time God is speaking with tough love, he is still quietly listening and mercifully offering grace. Even at this late hour (when the day of the Lord is near), his grace is still available. This tender love of God for his people is shown in his loving invitation. As the people stand silently before him, he says, "Gather together . . . O shameful nation, before the appointed time arrives and that day sweeps on like chaff, before the fierce anger of the Lord comes upon you, before the day of the Lord's wrath comes upon you. Seek the Lord, all you humble of the land, you who do what he commands. Seek righteousness, seek humility; perhaps you will be sheltered on the day of the Lord's anger" (2:1–3). What a tender invitation!

God is saying, come with others of like mind before the presence of the Lord and seek his face. Make *him* your ambition. Make knowing him your prime concern. Do what is right in his eyes. Be made right with him. Be humble instead of proud. Get rid of your self-sufficiency and arrogance.

Why didn't Jack Nicklaus ever throw another club? I think I know why—he knew his dad meant what he said. If he'd had the slightest inkling that his dad would say, "Oh, I didn't really mean it," Jack would still be petulantly throwing his clubs today. Instead, he's a self-controlled, capable, professional athlete with an admirable reputation. That's what God wants for each of his children. He invites us to step into true greatness—commitment to Christ and a life lived obediently under his direction.

God's Plan for His People

Look at God's plan for his people: " 'Then will I purify the lips of the peoples, that all of them may call on the name of the Lord and serve him shoulder to shoulder. From beyond the rivers of Cush my worshipers, my scattered people, will bring me offerings. On that day you will not be put to shame for all the wrongs you have done to me, because I will remove from this city those who rejoice in their pride. Never again will you be haughty on my holy hill. But I will leave within you the meek and humble, who trust in the name of the Lord. The remnant of Israel will do no wrong . . .' " (3:9–13).

What is he promising here? There will always be those who will stand out from the crowd of unbelievers. They will humble themselves, and seek the Lord. Asking for his forgiveness and his grace, they will respond to his tender loving call. They will find that they are a remnant, a minority in a society basically moving further and further away from God. In him they will find a new security, a new attitude.

Have you ever confronted the tough love of God, recognizing that he means what he says? Years ago God said to you, "You throw one more club and you will never set foot on my golf course again." And he meant it. Did you ever face up to his tough love? "Engage in that behavior one more time," he said, "and you will never set foot in my heaven." Did you believe it? Then you heard him say to be silent before him and come to him in repentance: "Humble yourself before me," said the Lord, "and I will give you a new heart. You will be part of the remnant of my people."

Have you done that? Or do you just shrug your shoulders and say, "He didn't mean it. That's Old Testament"? Let me ask you something. If that is just "Old Testament" and God doesn't take sin seriously, and doesn't judge sin, why does the New Testament have a cross? If the Old Testament is not to be taken seriously, why did Christ die? If God doesn't mean what he says, why then did Christ shed his precious blood?

Zephaniah ends with a rich expression of God's loving care: "On that day they will say to Jerusalem, 'Do not fear, O Zion; do not let your hands hang limp. The Lord your God is with you, he is mighty to save. He will take great delight in you, he will quiet you with his love, he will rejoice over you with singing' " (3:16, 17).

The feminist movement is trying to get us to view God as both father and mother. They insist on talking about him as "he" and "she." While I think much of this is sheer nonsense, they do have a case in verses like this. God is shown in all the tenderness of a mother caring for her tiny baby. Look at the picture again in this light. Have you ever seen a mother with a newborn baby, oblivious to everything, just taking great delight in her child? The baby becomes fussy and begins to cry. Maybe father is holding it for a moment—like a football. Mother takes her baby back and quiets him with her love. Then she begins to quietly sing a lullaby. The baby becomes quiet and peaceful—and the mother rejoices over her baby in love.

That is the picture we have here of the tender love of God. Which would you rather live with—a God who is your judge or a God who is your Savior? Whom would you rather meet? A God of righteous indignation—or a God who is like a mother with a small child, who receives you warmly, holds you securely, quiets you with his love, rejoices over you with singing? If you respond to his love as you ought, you will seek the Lord. If you respond to his love as you ought, you will seek righteousness. You will learn humility. You will seek shelter in him.

Jack Nicklaus's father got his son's attention with an act of tough but tender love. That is how God approaches us in this prophecy of Zephaniah.

T e n
FEAR GOD AND NOTHING ELSE
Haggai

THE BIBLE TALKS about fear in many different ways. Sometimes the word simply means to be emotionally distraught. When it talks about the fear of God, which the Bible says is "the beginning of wisdom," of course, it does not mean just being emotionally distraught. To fear God means simply to have a deep sense of reverence for him. It means to live in a continuous state of holy awe before him. People who live this way become what we sometimes call "God-fearers." They live their lives with reverence for what he says and a deep awareness of who he is. Accordingly, the very nature and character of their lives is different from those who are not God-fearers.

One of the delightful things that happens to people who are God-fearers is that they have a keenly developed sense of who God is and of what he is doing. They know that he is greater than their circumstances and grander than their problems. That is why I can say that if we fear God there is really nothing else to fear.

An old hymn, "All through the changing scenes of life," has this line: "Fear him, ye saints, and ye shall have nothing else to fear." Fear is a debilitating experience. In his classic sermon on fear, Clarence E. Macartney told the story of a peasant driving into a European city. The man was hailed by an aged woman who climbed up into his cart. As they drove along, the man became alarmed as he learned his passenger was the plague, cholera. But the old woman assured him that only ten people in the city would die of cholera. She even offered him a dagger, saying he could kill her if more than ten died. But after they reached the city, more than one hundred perished. As the angry peasant drew the dagger to deal a death blow, the old woman lifted her hand and protested, "Wait, I killed only ten. Fear killed the rest!"

Haggai's Message

Down through the centuries people have lived to a greater or lesser degree in fear. They fear the future, the present, and the consequences of the past. They fear the Communists, or they fear a recession. They may fear what is going to happen to their children. Many tend to live in a constant state of dread. They are emotionally distraught. Haggai has a message for such people—and for all of us. If we learn to fear God in the right way, there is nothing else to fear.

Don't misunderstand me. This expression does not fall into the same category with President Roosevelt's famous statement in 1933 when he said in his inaugural address with great flourish, "We have nothing to fear but fear itself." That's great rhetoric, but not too practical. What we do have to fear is a whole lot of things—unless we have something grander and greater to depend upon. That grander and greater entity is the Lord God Almighty, the great and glorious One who controls our circumstances.

What is happening in Haggai's world? The Assyrians have come from Nineveh and have overthrown Israel.

Subsequently, the Assyrians themselves have been over-thrown by the Babylonians. These fearsome people have attacked Judah and Jerusalem and conquered them, taking the people of Jerusalem into captivity. (The minor prophets, you remember, predicted that the Babylonians were coming and that God was going to use them to bring judgment upon Jerusalem.) Almost a century has elapsed between the time of the prophet Habakkuk and Haggai. During that time Jerusalem and Judah have fallen and the people of Judah have been in captivity for approximately seventy years. Then, after seventy years, the people are invited to leave Babylonia.

The Assyrians seemed unbeatable until along came the Babylonians and overthrew them. Judah was overthrown by the Babylonians—and now the Babylonians are con-quered by the Medes and the Persians. One of the Persian kings, Cyrus, decided that all the people who had been taken captive were to be released. An edict was issued and the captives were allowed to return to Jerusalem.

As they return (the story is told in Ezra and Nehemiah) we learn much about what they want to do. Seeing Jerusa-lem destroyed by the Babylonians, they were utterly devas-tated. There was nothing left for them; their God had given them the land and the holy city, Jerusalem, and in the center of his holy city was the magnificent temple, the focal point of their worship, but now all this, including Jerusalem, is in ruins.

At the site of the temple, not a stone is left lying upon another. The devastation is overwhelming. But the people have good leadership and they are encouraged to begin re-building.

One of the first things they want to do is to start worship-ing the Lord in the place of his appointment. So they build an altar. Because it is so inadequate, they start to rebuild the temple itself. But then they run into all kinds of prob-lems. One of their main sources of difficulty is the Assyri-ans, who have come to live in Palestine, mingling with the remnant of Israel, and intermarrying with the Jews. This alliance has produced a people called Samaritans. At first, these people wanted to join with the Jews in rebuilding the temple, but the people of Judah refused them. As a result, a deep animosity arose between the two, an animosity that lasted all through biblical times and is still very real today.

The Samaritans decided to terrorize this little band of Jews who were coming back, trying to rebuild Jerusalem and the temple, and the Jews became terrified of the Samaritans. They felt surrounded by enemies far more powerful than they, and they didn't know how to handle the situation. As a result, they took more notice of their enemies than they did of their all-powerful Lord. They became more aware of their circumstances than they were of the Lord who had restored them to the land as he had promised.

Two Threads

There are two threads in the prophetic message: (1) that the judgment of God will come, and (2) that there will always be blessing available.

Now they see God once again intervene in blessing. They become so engaged in what they are doing and so overwhelmed by what other people are doing that fear raises its ugly head. They begin to fear people more than they fear the Lord—and they receive all kinds of threats. In the end they are so threatened by the people around them that they stop the work of rebuilding the temple. Their enemies bring political pressure to bear, and the Jews find that they are forbidden by the political power structure to deal any further with the rebuilding project. It is rather obvious that they are concerned about their well-being, their own survival. They are concentrating on the material things. Putting that together with the political pressures and the fear of people around them, it is easy to understand why they halted the noble task of rebuilding the temple. Reinstituting that which made them unique, the worship of Jehovah, comes to an abrupt end in the face of their fear.

Against this background Haggai speaks. He sees fear on

every hand. The people have gone through decades of turmoil. They have just come out of seventy years of exile, and have seen great powers come and go. They have now come back and they think everything is going to be fine. But then they are confronted with this awesome power of the enemies around them. Surrounded, with nothing working their way, they are afraid they will not survive.

It is understandable that they are overcome with fear and paralyzed by circumstances. But the message of the Lord through Haggai is uncompromising. They have to learn to fear the Lord rather than people. They are to fear God rather than political pressure. Haggai speaks forcefully to this point.

Notice the emphasis he places on the nature of the Lord. It is demonstrated by a clear-cut acknowledgment of who he is. Haggai calls him "the Lord Almighty" four times in chapter 1 (vv. 2, 5, 7, 9).

Covered by Concern

That is, of course, a message the people of the restoration have forgotten. They have the Lord, but he is somewhat puny in their sight. He rates below political pressure and fear and concerns about poverty. He is not a Lord who transcends these things. In their thinking, he has been affected by these things. The Lord is great as long as they don't have any people fears. The Lord is mighty as long as they don't have any political pressures. The Lord is super as long as they are not poor. Should any of these come in, he is no longer a Lord greater than the objects of their fear and causes of concern.

How easy it is for us to become so engulfed by our concerns, so overwhelmed by our anxieties, that we are literally paralyzed by our fears. We have overlooked something: The Lord Almighty is still the Lord. To acknowledge this is the first step in the fear of the Lord. Second, as we begin to acknowledge who he is and take seriously what he says, we must be obedient to him. Notice what Haggai says. The people have been commissioned to go back and rebuild

Jerusalem, to repair the temple. But they say, " ' "The time has not yet come for the Lord's house to be built" ' " (1:2). God has given them a command, but, like the popular commercial says it, they have a better idea. They have decided to look after their own affairs first. Then they will deal with the affairs of the Lord. "Dead wrong!" says the Lord. "You deal with my affairs first and then I will look after your affairs."

Here again we encounter that age-old problem of God's people. So often we feel that if we can get our circumstances under control and in order, then, whatever we have left over, we can devote to the Lord. This is how we operate with our finances, for example. This is often how we utilize our time. We work out our budget and if there is anything left, we give it to the Lord. Or we look at our time commitments and decide what we are going to do with our time. Then, if there is any time left over, we will devote some of it to the Lord. This attitude shows itself in how we in the church work with our ministries. If we can fit some ministry in among all the other things, well and good.

This even happens on the Lord's day. It is ordained by the Lord specifically for his worship, but many people no longer treat it as a day of worship. They will worship if they can fit it in among all their other activities. But often we fail to put first things first.

We demonstrate our fear of the Lord by acknowledging who he is and doing what he says. What does he say? "Build my temple first. Get your priorities sorted out. Seek first the kingdom of God and his righteousness and all these other things will be added unto you." How easy it is for us to say, "Seek first all these other things, and if any time or energy or money is left over, then just send it to the kingdom."

God's Command

The fear of the Lord first enables me to acknowledge who he is. Then it requires me to act in obedience to what he says. Third, the fear of the Lord means *involvement in what he does.* " 'Is it a time for you yourselves to be living in your paneled houses, while this house remains a ruin?' " the Lord asks. The situation is clear. The people who have come back to Jerusalem out of exile want to build themselves nice homes. Not only that, they want to embellish them. But no one has lifted a finger in the rebuilding of the temple. Foundations were laid—but they have long been overgrown with weeds. Where there should be an edifice to the glory of God, there is nothing but grass and hoot owls. Absolutely nothing is going on there at all.

The People's Response

This much is clear. The people are not prepared to involve themselves in what God has called them to do. The fear of the Lord is always demonstrated by people who *obey* their Lord. These people are not obedient!

"This is what the Lord Almighty says: 'Give careful thought to your ways. You have planted much, but have harvested little. . . . Give careful thought to your ways' " (vv. 5, 7). "Take a good long look at your lifestyle," God says. "Consider your priorities. If you take a hard look at what you are doing, what will you discover?" Quite frankly we discover that the Lord doesn't rate too high on our list of priorities. We don't have that sense of reverence for him, that deep sense of awe in his presence. We have lost sight of the privilege of being God's people. We are uniquely called to be different, to do what nobody else is prepared to do. But we no longer desire what he desires. If we are going to demonstrate the fear of the Lord, we are going to submit ourselves to what he requires.

" 'Go up into the mountains,' " he tells them, " 'and bring down timber and build the house, so that I may take pleasure in it and be honored' " (1:8). Once again the Lord comes up with a clear-cut set of instructions. They must make a decision—to obey or not. These people have no fear of the Lord before their eyes. Their lives and their priorities demonstrate that. They are absorbed with their own homes and are perfectly happy letting the Lord's house lie in waste. They worship with their words but not with their hearts. This is the core of their problem. They don't fear the Lord, but they fear everything else.

What is it that hinders the fear of the Lord? One of the great hindrances is concentration on self rather than on God. The more I look at our society the more convinced I am that our fundamental problem is our increasing self-centeredness.

The "Me" Generation

Ours is the "me" generation. Remember Narcissus? He was that mythological Greek character who fell in love with his own reflection. To be narcissistic is to be totally and utterly absorbed with oneself. Our whole generation is becoming increasingly infatuated with its own image.

Look at the things that are of most interest to people today. Basically, they fall under one category—self-improvement. Self-satisfaction and self-gratification are the primary concerns of our narrow world. "I've got to be me!" "I must be fulfilled!" When that attitude prevails, we come apart at the seams.

Why are there so many abortions? Simply because many pregnant women are more interested in their own "rights" than they are about right or wrong. Why is there so much divorce? Usually because those who are involved in marital problems put their own well-being first.

What happens when we become God-centered? A different attitude emerges. God says, "Divorce do I hate," and we take what he says seriously! We also have an entirely different attitude toward abortion because we recognize that the life we are aborting was uniquely created by God. When we become God-centered we are concerned about who he is and what he says rather than about our own selfish interests.

A commitment to the material rather than the spiritual

is a phenomenal hindrance to the fear of the Lord. The idea of rebuilding the temple, the idea of reinstituting the worship that God had ordained, and for which he has specifically returned them to the land, is of relatively little importance to them. The thing that matters is to make sure that their own situation is secure.

On one occasion Jesus said, "Don't fear man who can only kill the body, but rather fear him who after he has killed the body can cast the soul into hell." Isn't it amazing how we get things out of perspective? This fear of man can unhinge us—but what is of paramount importance is our relationship to the living God. The thing that indicates the reality of our relationship with him, as opposed to our relationship to mankind, is whether we are more concerned about spiritual reality than material gain.

Clearly the people of the restoration are more committed to the material than they are to the spiritual. Their commitment to the Lord is being hindered because they have a commitment to extravagance rather than necessity. Note what Haggai asks them: " 'Is it a time for you yourselves to be living in paneled houses, while this house remains a ruin?' "

Clearly, they needed shelter. They needed a base from which to work. God is not denying them that at all. What he is objecting to is their unbelievable extravagance. They are simply heaping upon themselves one luxury after another. God is happy for them to have somewhere to be warm and sheltered, a place to raise their families. But now they must get on with building the house of the Lord. They are so intent on personal extravagance that they haven't even started God's house. It is overgrown with weeds. They make loud protestations of honoring the Lord—but in actual fact they are more interested in their own comforts.

They are also committed to excuses rather than reality. " 'The time has not yet come for the Lord's house to be built,' " (1:2) they say. "We will do it when the right time comes." The reality of the situation is this: God has told them the way to do it, but they have made an end run around what God says. Whenever we find ourselves more committed to excuses than to accepting the reality of doing things God's way, we have built up a tremendous roadblock to the fear and acknowledgment of the Lord. That acknowledgment requires recognition of who he is, obedience to what he says, involvement in what he does, desiring what he desires, and submission to what he requires.

Obedience Is the Key

God has an answer to this problem: "Then Zerubbabel son of Shealtiel, Joshua son of Jehozadak, the high priest, and the whole remnant of the people obeyed the voice of the Lord their God and the message of the prophet Haggai, because the Lord their God had sent him. And the people feared the Lord" (v. 12). What turned them around and brought them to the point of reality? They recognized Haggai for what he claimed to be, God's messenger. They listened to what he had to say, and they recognized it for what it was—God's message. As they heard God's message through God's messenger they demonstrated tremendous reverence for the voice of the Lord and they *obeyed* that voice.

One of the most exciting things we can do in our generation is affirm that God has given us his Word. He has raised up people who will commit themselves to the study of that Word and in the power of the Holy Spirit proclaim it to be true. It is not that they who do it are any different from others. It is that God has simply called and gifted them. He has appointed them for this particular task. As we hear God's Word through God's servants we can either say that it is not God's Word, that it is just their bias—or we can say, "Let us hear the voice of the Lord."

This does not mean that any preacher claims infallibility. We always need checks and balances. I fully expect people to check me out against the plain teachings of the Word. God's people must, with a deep reverence, hear the Word.

Anyone worth his salt as a preacher will make sure that the people are getting the Word of God. Then it is incumbent upon those people to rightly respond to what God says. One of the great things we can say about the people of the restoration is that they obeyed the voice of the Lord and feared him. This was the great turning point for them.

What happens as a result of this fear of God? They begin to exhibit a different attitude, and become involved in an entirely different project. This fearlessness is clearly explained by Haggai. First of all, it is related to their understanding of God's commitment to complete what he starts:

> On the twenty-first day of the seventh month, the word of the Lord came through the prophet Haggai: "Speak to Zerubbabel . . . [and] to Joshua . . . to the remnant of the people. Ask them, 'Who of you is left who saw this house in its former glory? How does it look to you now? Does it not seem to you like nothing? But now be strong, O Zerubbabel,' declares the Lord. 'Be strong, O Joshua. . . . Be strong, all you people of the land,' declares the Lord, 'and work. For I am with you,' declares the Lord Almighty. 'This is what I covenanted with you when you came out of Egypt. And my Spirit remains among you. Do not fear.'
>
> "This is what the Lord Almighty says: 'In a little while I will once more shake the heavens and the earth, the sea and the dry land. I will shake all nations, and the desired of all nations will come, and I will fill this house with glory,' says the Lord Almighty. 'The silver is mine and the gold is mine,' declares the Lord Almighty. 'The glory of this present house will be greater than the glory of the former house,' says the Lord Almighty. 'And in this place I will grant peace' . . ." (2:1-9).

What is God saying? Simply this: "I am committed to completing what I started." Let's look behind the scenes. As they start to rebuild the temple there are some very old people there. These folks remember when they were kids in the temple that Solomon built. That superb structure has been demolished, and now this little remnant of people has come back to rebuild a new temple. The young people are all excited, but the older ones sit there, and are crying. They say, "If only you kids remembered the former temple. This new one is pathetic. It doesn't belong in the same league." Then they begin to talk about the good old days with some degree of justification, because the new temple doesn't compare to Solomon's temple.

But then the Lord comes and speaks to these discouraged workers: "Don't be discouraged, because I have covenanted with you when you came out of Egypt always to be present among you. Don't be afraid. I'm going to triumph in the end. I will shake the nations, I'm going to build this temple, and it is going to be so glorious that the glory of this one will far surpass the former. And in it will be peace."

The Two Temples

As we look at it realistically, there is no way the temple these folks built could surpass the glory of Solomon's. But the scope and size of things has changed. God is speaking of shaking and controlling the nations. He says, "The desired of all nations will come."

It is rather obvious that Haggai is doing what the prophets do so often. He is telescoping the immediate and the ultimate—and there is a great gap between the two. He is looking right down through the ages and is talking about a new temple that God will build for his presence. He's talking about a new temple that he will build to bring "the desired of all nations." He is talking about a new temple that will be so full of his glory that people will not even believe it possible.

There is a sense in which the temple is the body of Christ now. The church of Jesus Christ is what Haggai had in mind. Though he probably doesn't understand it himself, Haggai is saying, "God is committed to completing what he began. What he began in the people of Israel he will bring into sharper focus in the church of Jesus Christ. But what he is doing in the church is a poor reflection of what he will ultimately do when he establishes his great, glorious, eternal kingdom."

Through Haggai God says to these distraught people: "Don't fear people, for I am the One who in Christ shall bring all things to full and total consummation." What a great message that is for God's people at all times. How do we become fearless? By fearing the Lord. When we fear the Lord, we fear a Lord who is committed to completing what he starts—and we know we are on the winning side.

Then another oracle comes: "On the twenty-fourth of the ninth month, in the second year of Darius, the word of the Lord came to the prophet Haggai: 'This is what the Lord Almighty says . . .' " (2:10, 11). Haggai explains this oracle, saying in effect, "Listen, do you think that consecration can be taught?" The answer is no. "Do you think all defilement is contagious?" And the answer is yes. "Do you realize," he then asks, "that you are engaging in things that are defiling the society and that your sin has all kinds of sociological consequences?" They say, "Yes, we do."

Listen and Learn

Haggai says, "Then listen. If you continue in this way you will bring more disaster upon yourselves. But if you live in obedience to God I promise you he will bless you. Take inventory of what you have here and I want you to remember something. Today is the day that you are going to recognize sin for what it is. You are going to turn from it and follow God. From this day on in a very special way the blessing of God will be on this community. Check me out and see if it isn't true."

God is saying, "Listen, I care for you. I care for them so much that I want them to do things my way. If you do things my way, you will discover the reality of my care and the blessing that will be heaped upon you."

When we fear the Lord we become fearless. Why? Because, first of all, we fear a Lord who is committed to completing what he began. Second, we fear a Lord who is committed to caring for those who are his. This brings us to the final oracle:

> The word of the Lord came to Haggai a second time. . . . I will overturn royal thrones and shatter the power of the foreign kingdoms. I will overthrow chariots and their drivers; horses and their riders will fall, each by the sword of his brother. 'On that day,' declares the Lord Almighty, 'I will take you, my servant Zerubbabel. . . . and I will make you like my signet ring, for I have chosen you,' declares the Lord Almighty" (2:20, 22, 23).

What is God saying? He is enunciating again his commitment to exalt his chosen people. There is no record that Zerubbabel became anyone important—but if you look in the genealogies of the New Testament you will discover something interesting. Zerubbabel was one of the forefathers of the Lord Jesus!

Why and how can we become fearless? When we fear the Lord. How can fearing the Lord take away the fear in my life? If I know that he is committed to completing what he started in my life, then I can rest secure. If I know that he is committed to caring for those who are his, I can rest secure in that promise. When I fear the Lord there is no need to fear anything else. What can man do to me if the Lord reigns in my life? What can the world do to me if the Lord reigns? The Apostle Paul answered it beautifully for us: "For to me, to live is Christ and to die is gain." That was why Paul was so fearless. We can have that same fearlessness.

E l e v e n
THE GOD WHO MAKES THINGS HAPPEN
Zechariah

IN THE APOCALYPTIC BOOK of Zechariah the prophet looks into the distant future. Because the book is so full of symbols, shapes, and images, it has been called "obscure." Like other prophetic visions, many of the things it describes will only be understood when the words are fulfilled.

In spite of its obscurity, however, Zechariah's broad themes are clear. With the prophet we can sense the gathering of mysterious forces and hear the thundering battles that seem for a time to promise victory of evil over good. Later we can sense the sudden joy as God intervenes to deliver Jerusalem. We rejoice with the prophet as the bitter mourning of the people is transformed into joy.

Zechariah is the longest and most mysterious of the minor prophets, and it is also the most difficult to understand. Zechariah seems to have a broader outlook than do the other minor prophets.

It is interesting to note, too, that Zechariah is grouped with Haggai as the most effective of the minor prophets: "So the elders of the Jews continued to build and prosper under the preaching of Haggai the prophet and Zechariah, a descendant of Iddo" (Ezra 6:14). Haggai and Zechariah played a major role in the dramatic turnaround of God's people. Zechariah gives his listeners a brief history lesson in the first six verses of chapter 1. Two months have elapsed since Haggai started ministering before Zechariah begins to speak. We have the specific dates in both Haggai and Zechariah. In the early verses of the first chapter, we see that Zechariah is speaking to a somewhat dispirited, rather lax people. They have been liberated from their exile after seventy years and have returned to their promised land with the expressed intent of establishing the city of God, Jerusalem, where they are in the process of rebuilding the temple and reclaiming the land for the Lord. They started out well—but now they have become discouraged.

Because of their discouragement, they have decided that they will concentrate on their own interests without concern for the things of the Lord. At this point, you remember, Haggai spoke to them, telling them it was not right that they should be spending all their time on their own houses, on beautifying their own lives while the house of the Lord lay in total disrepair. They had simply laid the foundations for that house—and for fifteen years had done nothing further.

Zechariah addresses this same problem. He points out to the people not only what the situation is, but also reminds them that the reason their enemies are triumphing around them is that they have been living in disobedience to God. They find themselves in all kinds of problems as far as the land is concerned—and as far as God's purposes being worked out in their lives is concerned.

Zechariah amplifies this problem in chapter 7:

Then the word of the Lord Almighty came to me: "Ask all the people of the land and the priests, 'When you fasted and mourned in the fifth and seventh months for the past seventy years, was it really for me that you fasted? And when you were eating and drinking, were you not just feasting for yourselves? Are these not the words the Lord proclaimed through the earlier prophets when Jerusalem and its surrounding towns were at rest and prosperous, and the Negev and the western foothills were settled?' "

And the word of the Lord came again to Zechariah: "This is what the Lord Almighty says: 'Administer true justice; show mercy and compassion to one another. Do not oppress the widow or the fatherless, the alien or the poor. In your hearts do not think evil of each other.'

"But they refused to pay attention; stubbornly they turned their backs and stopped up their ears. They made their hearts as hard as flint and would not listen to the law or to the words that the Lord Almighty had sent by his Spirit through the earlier prophets. So the Lord Almighty was very angry.

" 'When I called, they did not listen; so when they called, I would not listen,' says the Lord Almighty. 'I scattered them with a whirlwind . . .' " (7:4–14).

Notice what Zechariah is doing here. He is pointing out that the conditions in the city of God are not right. The temple which ought to have been rebuilt stands in ruins. The people have become dispirited, lax in their spiritual experience. He points out how, historically, the situation can be directly attributed to the laxity of their forefathers and their own disobedience. Unless they are very careful, he says, they are going to get themselves back in exactly the same position.

The German philosopher Hegel is supposed to have said, "If history teaches us anything, it teaches us that it doesn't teach us anything." That's a rather cynical view, to which I do not personally adhere; but there is an element of truth in it.

When I was a boy, my math teacher Danny Jackson used to say, "Learn by making mistakes. But don't make the same mistakes twice." Then he would turn to me in front of the whole class: "Briscoe," he would say, "you are great at making mistakes—but you go on making the same mistakes. You never learn!" History teaches us that we go on making the same mistakes too, because we don't learn from our mistakes.

Zechariah, in the name of the Lord, speaks to God's people and says, "Please study your history. Check on what has happened. Look at the mistakes that you have made. Look at the sins that are being committed. Look at what God has done—and then have the sense to recognize that you are going exactly the same way your forefathers did. Will you never learn?"

Our Tendency to Forget

Zechariah is bringing a powerful message. In his second epistle, Peter tells the people to whom he is writing that he is not telling them anything new. Rather, he wants to stimulate their minds by reminding them of what he has already taught them. Why? Because we have a remarkable propensity to forget—a striking capacity to overlook—a built-in ability to ignore the things that God has already shown us. Zechariah's message to each of us is this: *Please learn from your own history.* If not, *learn from what happened to your parents.* If not that, *look what happened to previous generations of believers.* Look at world history and see that over and over again the same mistakes have been made. Beware lest you in your own spiritual life fall into the same trap. That's the gist of the first part of Zechariah.

Zechariah's Visions

In the second part the prophet gives us a rather lengthy account of his eight visions. I believe all of them came on one occasion. One after another, these dramatic, colorful visions came pounding in on his consciousness. We won't try to cover them all in detail, but let's note them briefly. They are found in chapters 1 through 6.

The first one is the vision of the horseman and four different colored horses. He asks the angel he sees in the vision, "What are these, my Lord?" The angel seems somewhat surprised that Zechariah doesn't know, but he tells him anyway that these are the messengers who have gone out and are now returned to report what they have seen. They say that there seems to be peace and prosperity all around the area in which Zechariah is ministering, and this is a difficult thing for them to accept. They are looking for the blessing of God, but as far as they are concerned, nothing is working. Things just aren't coming together the way they expected, so they are asking the question, "Why aren't we seeing things happen the way we think they should?"

The question is not answered at this particular point, although God does remind them that he is going to carry out his purposes. This leads straight into the second set of symbols, four horns and four blacksmiths. These are huge steel horns that were the symbol of power and strength— not musical instruments.

"What are these four horns?" the prophet asks. "These are the forces that have scattered Judah and Israel and Jerusalem," replies the angel. They are symbolic of the forces arrayed against God and his purposes.

Depressed, discouraged, and dispirited, the people ask why everything is going great for everyone else and not for them. They are reminded of an important truth: All the enemies, all the horns raised up against them, will be battered into pulp by the blacksmiths that God will raise up. God will be their Savior.

A Man with a Measuring Line

This is the message that is coming through to the people of God. First of all, it answers their question about why things aren't going so well, reminding them that God is working out his purpose behind the scenes. Eventually, all their enemies will be overthrown.

The third vision comes at the beginning of chapter 2, a vision of a man with a measuring line.

"Where are you going?" asks Zechariah. He answers, "To measure Jerusalem, to find out how wide and how long it is" (2:2). The angel then begins to help explain the whole situation: " 'Jerusalem will be a city without walls because of the great number of men and livestock in it. And I myself will be a wall of fire around it,' declares the Lord, 'and I will be its glory within. . . . Many nations will be joined with the Lord in that day and will become my people. I will live among you and you will know that the Lord Almighty has sent me to you. . . . Be still before the Lord, all mankind, because he has roused himself from his holy dwelling,' " the prophet declares (2:4, 5, 11, 13).

Zechariah is its own best commentary. Later on, the Lord speaks through Zechariah and says: " 'I am very jealous for Zion [another word for Jerusalem]; I am burning with jealousy for her.' This is what the Lord says: 'I will return to Zion and dwell in Jerusalem. Then Jerusalem will be called the City of Truth, and the mountain of the Lord Almighty will be called the Holy Mountain.' . . . 'Once again men and women of ripe old age will sit in the streets of Jerusalem, each with cane in hand because of his age. The city streets will be filled with boys and girls playing there' " (8:1–5).

The prophet goes on: " 'Many peoples and the inhabitants of many cities will yet come, and the inhabitants of one city will go to another and say, "Let us go at once to entreat the Lord and seek the Lord Almighty. I myself am going." And many peoples and powerful nations will come to Jerusalem to seek the Lord Almighty and to entreat him.' This is what the Lord Almighty says: 'In those days ten men from all languages and nations will take firm hold of one Jew by the edge of his robe and say, "Let us go with

you, because we have heard that God is with you" ' "
(8:20–23).

A Vision for the Minority

What does this vision say? Zechariah is reminding the
people that God is committed to overthrowing their enemies. He is projecting into the future and saying, "God is
going to demonstrate that Jerusalem and Zion are his dwelling place. Not only that, his dwelling place will become
so powerful, so rich, so glorious, and so wonderful that
people from all over the world will want to congregate there.
Because they will recognize the glory of the Lord and the
wonder of his work among his people, they will seek to
share the blessing themselves."

Remember, Zechariah is speaking to a depressed minority.
Struggling to survive against all their enemies, they can't
even succeed in getting the temple built. But God is speaking a positive message of hope. He is telling them, "I'm
going to make things happen, and you had better believe
it." This is the thrust of Zechariah.

The Fourth Vision

The fourth vision concerns Joshua the high priest, ". . .
standing before the angel of the Lord, and Satan standing
at his right hand to accuse him. The Lord said to Satan,
'The Lord rebuke you, Satan! The Lord, who has chosen
Jerusalem, rebuke you! Is not this man a burning stick
snatched from the fire?'

"Now Joshua was dressed in filthy clothes as he stood
before the angel. The angel said to those who were standing
before him, 'Take off his filthy clothes.' Then he said to
Joshua, 'See, I have taken away your sin, and I will put
rich garments on you.' . . . ' "Listen, O high priest Joshua
and your associates seated before you, who are men symbolic
of things to come: I am going to bring my servant, the
Branch. . . . I will remove the sin of this land in a single
day" ' " (3:1–4, 8, 9).

For further commentary on this vision turn to chapter 6: " 'Take the silver and gold and make a crown, and set it on the head of the high priest, Joshua. . . . "Here is the man whose name is the Branch, and he will branch out from his place and build the temple of the Lord" ' " (vv. 11, 12).

The representative of the people is being accused by Satan. Since he is covered with filthy rags, it is obvious that he is in dire straits. He is representative of the people who have come out of exile. But now God says through the angel, "Take off his filthy garments. We will cleanse him. Not only will we cleanse him, we will give him the opportunity of facing up to a new challenge. He is going to lead the people in the way that they are supposed to go. Moreover, he is going to become a symbol of the Branch, a symbol of one much greater and grander than himself."

The high priest was to make continual offerings for sin. But this passage of Scripture tells us that this high priest is symbolic of one called the Branch who will take away the sin of the people in one single day. We begin to see that Zechariah is projecting even further into the future— clearly making a statement concerning One who would be the Messiah. In himself in one single act, the Messiah will take away the sin of the world.

The Messiah Crowned

In chapter 6, Zechariah introduces a strange idea: the high priest would be crowned. This is another clear projection concerning the coming Messiah. The strange visions of Zechariah begin to speak even more forcibly to the people. They are discouraged, but are reminded that God will overthrow their enemies. They begin to sense that God is going to do a work in Jerusalem so grand and so great that it will be beyond their comprehension. They recognize that he's going to cleanse and restore them, sending through them One who will be their Messiah. This One will take

away all their sins in one day, and give them the opportunity
to be what they have never been before. He will not only
be their priest; he will be their king.

The Gold Lampstand and the Two Olive Trees

A theme is developing through all these visions. Now
the prophet sees a lampstand and various lights, with all
kinds of pipes going from the reservoir in the lampstand
up to the lights. Two pipes run straight into the olive trees
from the lampstand. If you can figure out the exact meaning
of this obscure passage, you may be the first person to do
so. There are innumerable theories concerning its meaning.
We can be sure that this vision symbolizes a spiritual truth.
Zechariah asks, "What are those two olive trees?" and the
angel replies, "They are God's two anointed ones." What
are they doing? They are recognizing the power of God's
anointing upon them; from them is flowing that which enables God's glory to shine.

Interpreters have expressed different ideas about the identity of these two anointed ones. It seems obvious to me
that, in the immediate context, the two men would be Zerubbabel and Joshua, who are leading the people. According
to the text, the anointed ones must be men on whom the
power of God rested. Through them the sheer power of
God was going to flow to complete what he wanted to do
so that his glory could shine.

As further support for this, we've already seen that Joshua
is to be crowned, and that Zerubbabel is the one through
whom Christ should come. Now we see these two anointed
ones being made one. Note this great statement of God:
" 'Not by might nor by power, but by my Spirit,' says the
Lord Almighty" (4:6).

What will be accomplished in Jerusalem—not only immediately, but subsequently in the outworking of God's purposes—is not going to be done through might or military
power. It is not going to be done through human ingenuity.

Rather, it is going to be done by the direct power of the Spirit of God picking up his anointed people and working through them.

Assembling all these pictures, we now see that they build one upon the other. And a great lesson is coming across to the people in Zechariah's time. It is this: "You dispirited, discouraged people, surrounded by your enemies—asking why your enemies are doing so well, and you are doing so poorly—remember this! God will overthrow your enemies. He is going to finish his work of rebuilding Jerusalem far beyond anything you ever envisioned. He is going to cleanse you and work through you, bringing from you a Messiah who will take away all sin in a single day. He is going to do all this through the people he raised up—not through armies, not through human ingenuity, but through a people who recognize the sheer dynamic of his Spirit at work." This is the message they need to hear.

The Final Four Visions

Another vision unfolds. The prophet sees an open scroll, some thirty feet long by fifteen feet wide, on which are written two of the commandments, representing the Law's teaching of duty to God and neighbor. These words are called a "curse," for God has promised to punish all who refuse to obey. Now the words fly through the land, to actively carry out the Lord's judgment on sinners.

Beginning at Zechariah 5:5, the prophet sees wickedness personified. It is a woman locked in a large container used to measure out grain. Powerless, this wickedness is carried away to Babylon by two angels. Earlier, God's people had been carried captive to Babylon because of their wickedness. In the future, God will separate his people from evil—the evil will be taken captive and sent far away.

The final visions concern the angelic patrols that cover the earth. They ride in war chariots and sweep out over the world. A report comes back that "those going toward the north country have given my Spirit rest in the land

of the north" (6:8). In Bible prophecy, the "north" repre-
sents the nations and power of evil (see Joel 2:20, Ezekiel
38, 39). The rest God's Spirit now enjoys indicates that
these enemies have been defeated. The enemy having been
defeated, Zechariah is told to approach Joshua the high
priest, taking gold and silver to shape a royal crown. The
Hebrew word for "crown" is always used of a royal crown,
never of the priest's headdress.

According to Zechariah 3:8, Joshua stands symbolically
for "things to come"—especially for the promised Branch
(Messiah). The picture is of a union between the offices
of priest and king in the person of a single individual. When
he appears to "be a priest on his throne," the final and
true temple of the Lord will be erected (see Zech. 6:13).

At this point, the royal crown Zechariah shapes is to
be placed in the temple as a reminder of this prophecy
and as a testimony of the One who is to come.

It is interesting to wonder how much of this information
Zechariah and his contemporaries understood. More to the
point, however, we need to ask ourselves how much of
this ancient message is understandable and applicable in
our day. As we do not think in apocalyptic terms we find
the visions strange and unsettling, or just plain boring. But
when this information is studied carefully and reverently
in the light of other Scriptures there is much to cheer and
to challenge the modern believer.

Two Oracles of Encouragement

At chapter 9, Zechariah begins to look into the future.
This section, chapters 9 through 14, forms the second part
of the book and is filled with Messianic symbols and statements having to do with the end of the age. The prophet
looks to the day when the Lord will set up his earthly
kingdom, restoring Israel and judging the other nations.

Scholars have noted an abrupt change in the writing style
at this point in the book and some of them believe that
another man—not Zechariah—is responsible for what we

find there. Regardless of how you feel about that, I believe this prophecy is in the Bible for our encouragement as well as for that of Zechariah's contemporaries. It reminds us that God is working things out and is committed to his final purposes. We should never allow critical questions raised by honest scholarship to divert our attention from the devotional and practical application of God's Word to our lives. But, by the same token, we should not close our minds to the things which the scholars discover if they lead to an enhanced knowledge of the truth.

The "Ah-So" Day

I believe that a great and glorious day is coming. I call it the great "Ah-so" day. That day will come when God gathers us around his throne in glory. As we sit cross-legged there before him, he will explain the whole thing to us— and there will be a great cosmic, "Ah! So that's what you meant!" What an interesting day that will be.

Yes, we have to admit that there could be a change of authorship here—and there are definite problems with specific dating for the second half of Zechariah. But there is no problem about the Messianic content of this part of Zechariah. The latter part of Zechariah is a favorite source of material for the New Testament writers. Zechariah is quoted throughout the New Testament—even if some of the writers do attribute what he said to Jeremiah (as in Matthew 27:9, 10 which refers to Zechariah 11:12, 13).

Zechariah 9 through 11 gives the first oracle of encouragement. This passage seems to refer to the times of turmoil that come immediately after Israel's defeat and captivity. The Persians had overpowered the Babylonians who had carried the people of Jerusalem into exile, and it was they who subsequently allowed them to return to their homeland. Under Cyrus, the Persians built a massive empire that lasted some two hundred years, until Alexander the Great came on the scene.

At twenty years of age, in 336 B.C., Alexander was a great

king. He began one military campaign that lasted for eight years and in that time he built an empire greater than that of the Assyrians, Babylonians, and Persians combined. His was the most vast empire you can imagine, stretching all the way to India and up into what we now call Russia. From Greece it extended to North Africa where Alexander named a city after himself, Alexandria.

In the end, as a young man of thirty-three, Alexander reportedly sat down and cried because there were no other lands left to conquer. He was a tragic figure; he died defeated by his own greatness. Through his exploits, the culture of Greece spread across the then-known world, providing the perfect vehicle for spreading the gospel. The Greek language became the universal language. The New Testament, written in Greek, could go everywhere, and so all the world heard the gospel. God was working out his purposes even through a godless man like Alexander the Great. There is a flip side to this truth: Along with the Greek language spread the Greek culture, with all its aberrations. This created problems.

It seems that Zechariah is looking down the halls of history to see how God will overthrow the aberrations of Greek culture. How is he going to do it? Through a remarkable personage described in Zechariah 9:9. There Zechariah declares words now familiar. "Rejoice greatly, O Daughter of Zion! Shout, daughter of Jerusalem! See, your king comes to you, righteous and having salvation, gentle and riding on a donkey, and on a colt, the foal of a donkey." Doesn't that sound like Palm Sunday? It refers to the remarkable arrival of a king who will not be characterized by mighty armies and great white horses, but by humility and a servant attitude. His arrival in the holy city, meek and lowly, riding on a donkey, symbolizes his spirit.

What is Zechariah predicting? He is prophesying the overthrow of all the bad effects of the spreading Greek culture. This One is the exact opposite of all that the Greek empire stood for. Humility and meekness were his characteristics, which to the Greeks were marks of weakness. Our Lord Jesus comes, the appointed king, and overthrows all that Greece stands for. His nature, his teaching, and his sacrifice are direct contradictions to the Greek idea of power.

Incidentally, Jesus is still doing this today. Our modern world is permeated by much of Greek culture—only Christ can overthrow it.

The last five chapters of Zechariah are an uncannily accurate foreshadowing of the experiences of Jesus at the time of his earthly ministry. Fittingly, Zechariah uses the terms "shepherd" and "king" as a picture or symbol of the Messiah. And in these poetic last chapters the author pictures for us those events usually considered the end times. Chapters 9 through 11 describe the coming king and the jubilation in Jerusalem when he enters the city. The deceitful leaders are removed (10:2, 3) and the restoration of the city is welcomed.

Then a difficult interlude occurs. When the good shepherd comes on the scene to lead his flock, he is rejected out of hand. In turn for his paying the ransom and his guidance (even ridding the city of false shepherds), he is despised by the sheep, Judah. When the shepherd confronts the flock about their attitude he tells them to pay him what they feel he is worth. They establish his price at only "thirty pieces of silver" (11:12), the amount set in the Law as payment when a slave is accidentally killed (see Exodus 21:32). This is such an insult that the Lord commands that this "blood money" be thrown into the house of the Lord to "the potter," himself the most lowly artisan, who made the least valuable of vessels.

In the Gospels, of course, this passage is presented as a prophecy about Jesus who came announcing himself as the Good Shepherd (John 10:15–18). As the Bible makes clear, Jesus was rejected by those he came to save—but his death and resurrection were unmistakably a part of God's plan of redemption for man.

The second segment of apocalyptic teaching in Zechariah

appears in chapters 12 through 14. It again pictures jubilation in Israel at a time when all the nations of the world gather against Jerusalem and Judah. This is when God acts to finalize his plan for Judah, for the ultimate ransom paid those arrayed against her. The narrative covers the mourning for the One who was slain (the Messiah), the rejection of deceitful leaders, the scattering of the sheep, the great cataclysm in Jerusalem and, finally, the worship of God in the holy city with all the nations gathered to pay him homage.

As we look back over the eventful chapters of Zechariah, we can but marvel at this "God who makes things happen." There is so much in this prophecy that merits our attention, but limits of space preclude a fuller treatment. Suffice it to say that Zechariah, along with his colleagues, had such a sense of God's interest and involvement in human affairs that he could not only attribute contemporary events to divine activity but was also convinced that, ultimately, human affairs would find their consummation in the cosmic triumph of the Eternal One.

This sense of divine majesty and power, righteousness, and justice needs to be recaptured in the modern church so that we can take God seriously. But this sense of his authority must always be joined to the knowledge of his love and grace shown in the Good Shepherd who gave his life for the sheep.

Twelve
THE GOD WHO DOES NOT CHANGE
Malachi

WE ARE TOLD that variety is the spice of life. And many believe that old adage. The problem is: People who want to live the spicy life have overlooked the fact that a diet of spices can make you ill very quickly. One characteristic of modern society is that we are into variety all of the time. Those who produce the TV shows know this. They are constantly switching camera positions so as to vary the angle of our viewing and keep us watching. And if we grow tired of what is on the screen, we change channels. We are into change.

There was a time when preachers could speak for two or three hours—and no one would get up to leave. Now people become very concerned if a preacher speaks longer than "the allotted time." In pastors' conferences, when I tell the people that I normally preach for forty-five minutes, I'm usually greeted with total incredulity. My hearers can't believe our people will tolerate such lengthy preaching.

This is the kind of attitude being generated in our society. This doesn't mean, of course, that I'm against variety; it doesn't mean that I'm against doing things differently or that I'm opposed to change. But one thing that I am definitely opposed to is our forgetting that there are basic, fundamental principles upon which we must build our lives. We must constantly return to these foundational truths—or lose our moorings.

By all means, add a dash of spice. But please don't give me a diet of nothing but spices. By all means, keep variety coming—but make certain that there are constants upon which I can rely.

This is certainly true as far as our relationship with God is concerned. Even in worship experiences, there is an increasing clamor for more variety. Through Malachi, God has something to say to this obsession with variety. " 'I the Lord do not change' " (3:6).

If we are going to have stability in our lives, not only must we recognize that stable factors must be built into them; we have to recognize the fundamental truth: God himself does not change. I call this the keynote thought of the Book of Malachi.

Because of who he is and because of his unchanging nature we can have hope of stability in our lives. This is the underlying theme of Malachi, the twelfth of the minor prophets. Malachi is placed last among the twelve books and was probably the latest one of them to be written as well. We don't know the exact date when Malachi wrote his book. The temple had been rebuilt after a long and terrible period, as we have seen. Both Israel and Judah had fallen and gone into captivity. After their release they had come back to Jerusalem to rebuild the city and the temple. And because they had become discouraged in that ministry, the minor prophets came along to bolster their courage. After much struggle the city and the temple were rebuilt. Now the captivity has ended, defeat is in the past, the temple has been refurbished, and the restoration is complete. Everything is going according to plan.

That's the problem. Everything is going so smoothly that the people have become bored. In their boredom, they have become quite belligerent. It is Malachi's job to shock them back to reality. What is their response? They argue with God. "How have you loved us? How have we despised your name?" the people ask. There is an aura of discontent, an air of grumbling. Why is that?

Bored and Belligerent

When a group of people face a common enemy, they work wonderfully well together. But as soon as that enemy is defeated, or a common objective achieved, they begin grumbling and growling among themselves. The attitude of the people in Malachi's day was quite different from that when they faced hostile opposition. This disgruntled attitude is typical of people who "have it made" or who have it too good. The smoother things are going in general, the more likelihood there is of someone's becoming bored and belligerent. When that happens, we need to remind people that God does not change. We should center our attention on him. He is constant. And if our eyes are on him, we can handle all the pressures that come upon us. If we get our eyes off him, then tension and friction begin to arise. We need to remember that God does not change.

God's Love

There are at least six ways in which this is true. First of all, God's love does not change. Malachi begins his prophecy by declaring that the Lord says, " 'I have loved you.' "

He wants the people to remember that one thing is constant. The unchanging God is unchanging in his love toward his people.

But the very next phrase indicates Israel's reaction: " 'But you [the people] ask, "How have you loved us?" ' " (1:2). When people question God's love, they are spiritually at a low ebb. Have we modern-day Christians ever questioned God's love? If things don't go the way we want them to, how do we react? What about God's timing? Does God not do things when we want them done? We must look beyond our circumstances at God's revelation of himself. And when we do we see that he has set his unchanging love upon us. God answers their question, "How have you loved us?" by saying, " 'Was not Esau Jacob's brother?' . . . 'Yet I have loved Jacob, but Esau I have hated . . .' " (vv. 2, 3). This is a difficult passage to understand.

God is not referring here just to the twin boys, Jacob and Esau. Remember, even before their birth they began fighting each other in their mother's womb. Against all tradition, God chose the younger over the older son. Jacob would be the one who would become Israel. From Jacob the children of Israel would come, forming God's own special people. It was his arbitrary choice. God in his sovereignty is free to make arbitrary choices. His Messiah would come from one strain; he could not come from two.

Who is better suited to make an arbitrary choice than God himself? In making this choice, God says that he is demonstrating his special love for Israel. "I have chosen Israel as my covenant people," he says. By contrast, Esau's descendants have not been chosen as God's special people. Does this mean that God has chosen some for salvation and some for condemnation? No, he is not willing that *any* should perish. What he is saying is that he has chosen Israel to be the medium of his special blessing.

In effect God is saying to these descendants of Israel: "You must recognize that down through your long history I have stood firm with you. I have constantly demonstrated my love to you. Sometimes it's been a tough love, but I have repeatedly warned you that tough love was poured out upon you. Sometimes it has been a very tender love. You've always been sure of this: If you would respond to what I was saying, I would respond to you."

God could have said, "Listen, don't just look at Edom

and what has happened to them. Look at the Assyrians. Where are they? Remember when you were frightened of them? Look at the Babylonians. Where are they? Remember when you were frightened of them? Remember the Medes and the Persians. Where are they? Remember when you were frightened of them?"

God could go right down through history asking the same question: "What about the Greeks and the Romans? They have all come and gone. Yet I have set my love upon Israel and I have demonstrated the fact that my love is unchanging."

This is a simple message to God's people: "When you are in Christ, you are elect, chosen. You're locked in to all the eternal purposes of God and you can be sure of this—having exercised your free will in response to God's sovereign grace, you're the beneficiary of his love. And his love is unchanging. Don't look at your immediate circumstances to determine whether or not God loves you. Rather, look at the character of God revealed in the Scriptures. See his faithfulness to his sovereign choice. See his faithfulness to his sovereign grace. Therein be reminded again of his love."

But remember that God was disappointed. Did he find reciprocating love among his people? No, they are bored with him and they are belligerent toward him. They are grumbling and questioning at every point.

This must be one of the greatest disappointments to the heart of God. In spite of his consistent love for his people, they do not love him in return. So, the first thing we notice is that God does not change in terms of his love.

God's Glory

Moving to verse 6, we see that God has something further to say: " 'A son honors his father, and a servant his master. If I am a father, where is the honor due me? If I am a master, where is the respect due me?' . . . 'It is you, O priests, who despise my name. But you ask, "How have we despised your name?" You place defiled food on my altar. But you ask, "How have we defiled you?" ' "

At the end of this confrontation comes this dramatic conclusion: " 'For I am a great king,' says the Lord Almighty, 'and my name is to be feared among the nations' " (v. 14). God is now making a statement concerning his own glory. "I am a great king," he says. There is a sense in which God's intervention on behalf of his people clearly demonstrated his majestic glory and power. The ironic thing, however, is that the people of God, who should have been the first to acknowledge him, are the ones who seem unprepared to give him glory.

"I am getting no respect from my people," says God. "You are not glorifying my name as you ought." He is referring to the poor quality of worship among his people. "A great king can expect his subjects to respond to his majesty; a great father can expect his sons to be responsive to his fatherhood; and a master who looks after his servants well can expect servants to be responsive to his leadership," God says.

> "You place defiled food on my altar. . . . By saying that the Lord's table is contemptible. When you bring blind animals for sacrifice, is that not wrong? When you sacrifice crippled or diseased animals, is that not wrong? Try offering them to your governor! Would he be pleased with you? Would he accept you?" says the Lord Almighty.
>
> "Now implore God to be gracious to us. With such offerings from your hands, will he accept you?"—says the Lord Almighty.
>
> "Oh, that one of you would shut the temple doors, so that you would not light useless fires on my altar! I am not pleased with you," says the Lord Almighty. (vv. 7–10)

What a powerful statement!
The people have gone to great pains to rebuild the temple

and reinstitute the worship services—but God is dissatisfied with their empty ritual. Part of the ritual, of course, was the sacrifice of animals to the Lord. Only the best were to be sacrificed, but the people are saying, "We've got to sacrifice to the Lord again, but what can we find?" They hunt around among the flock to find some old sheep that is blind or lame—and bring it for a sacrifice. And the priest doesn't say anything. He sacrifices the animal as if it were perfect.

An old sheep staggering around on its last legs was not what God had in mind. "But," the people say, "this old thing is going to die anyway; let's sacrifice it to the Lord."

What is God's reaction? He says, "You do not honor the Lord by second-rate worship! You do not honor the Lord by fitting him into your schedule. And you do not honor the Lord by confessing to live sacrificially before him when in fact there is no sacrifice whatsoever."

This is the Lord's main concern at this point. And he lays the blame for this sacrilege fairly and squarely at the door of the priests: " 'And now this admonition is for you, O priests. If you do not listen, and if you do not set your heart to honor my name.' . . . 'I will send a curse upon you, and I will curse your blessings. Yes, I have already cursed them, because you have not set your heart to honor me' " (2:1, 2). God goes on to explain that the responsibility of the priests is not to let things slide as far as the people are concerned. Their responsibility is to teach the people, and lead them to make their hearts right with God. When they are right with God, they may then offer acceptable sacrifices.

The priests, however, have been turning blind eyes to the empty ritual going on around them. Indeed, they are part of it. They care nothing about the heart condition of the people. Now the Lord admonishes them: "You have not set your heart to honor me."

This is always the word of truth to God's people—particularly when they are bored with God. When worship and service no longer excite us, it is easy to let everything slide. Less important things take precedence; the service and worship of God are demoted to a "back burner" in our lives.

"This will not do!" says the Lord. Going through the motions of worship and service do not satisfy him. We must set our hearts to honor the Lord. How do we fail in this? Sometimes in the way we sing the hymns; sometimes in the way we teach the classes for which we've accepted responsibility; sometimes in the way we fail to follow through on our commitments. Something more interesting and exciting comes along—and we clearly show where our true commitments are.

God says, "This will not do. I am a great king, and I will be honored among the nations. If I'm a great king, I expect my subjects to honor me."

It is possible to be a dissembler in the church. Some serve out of wrong motivation, for recognition and honor. Some put on a vain show of worship, and then become bored with the whole thing. They settle back in a comfortable rut. When we get this way, we do not honor the Lord. We cannot bring our leftovers to him. But even if we do— his glory isn't changed. We may not feel loved, but God's love is the same. We may not feel like worshiping, but that is irrelevant—for God's glory remains unchanged.

God's Faithfulness

We have seen that God's love is unchanging. And his glory is ever the same. Now we turn to a third truth— God's faithfulness does not change either: "Have we not all one Father?" Malachi asks. "Did not one God create us? Why do we profane the covenant of our fathers by breaking faith with one another?" The Lord goes on to explain the ways in which faith has been broken. One thing, in particular, he finds totally unacceptable.

Another thing you do: You flood the Lord's altar with tears. You weep and wail because he no longer pays attention to your offerings or accepts them with pleasure from your hands. You ask, "Why?" It is because the Lord is acting as the witness between you and the wife of your youth, because you have broken faith with her, though she is your partner, the wife of your marriage covenant.

Has not the Lord made them one? In flesh and spirit they are his. And why one? Because he was seeking godly offspring. So guard yourself in your spirit, and do not break faith with the wife of your youth.

"I hate divorce," says the Lord God of Israel, "and I hate a man's covering himself with violence as well as with his garment," says the Lord Almighty. (vv. 13–16)

This is another powerful statement from the Lord. The men of Israel have been told to keep themselves quite separate from the pagan women around them, but they are not only disobeying that command and marrying these women; some of the Jews are actually divorcing their Jewish wives to do so! Casual divorces have become the normal and accepted practice. But God says categorically: "I utterly detest it." Why? Because he is a faithful God. He has made a covenant with his people and being a faithful God, he expects his people to be faithful to the covenants they have made.

After I have made a covenant with God, the greatest commitment I can make is to stand before God and make a covenant with my wife—for better or for worse, for richer or for poorer, in sickness and in health, till death do us part. That is the highest covenant after my covenant with God. One thing that God detests among his people is for people to overlook the fact that the basis of our relationship with him is faithfulness to a covenant. On the human level, one of the best ways to demonstrate that we understand faithfulness is by being faithful to the marriage commitment.

Where is the problem? The people have become bored. Their marriages are not working out the way they think they should; they are encountering difficulties; so they have decided they have cause to cancel their marriage commitment and enjoy themselves.

We hear over and over again, even among God's people at the present time, this idea: "God wants me to be happy. God wants my life to be fulfilled. He wants me to really enjoy life. I'm sure that this is what he is like." If people agree with that assessment, they go on to say, "I'm not happy in my marriage. Therefore, God wouldn't want me to stay in this situation. He wants me out of it." Thus they justify their actions.

There is something more important than our happiness. God wants us to do what is right. There is something right about being faithful to a covenant.

I heard somebody say recently, "The church of Jesus Christ today is governed more by psychology than theology."

Psychology has to do with how I feel about myself. Theology has to do with what God says about himself. And what God says about himself is: "I am a covenant-keeping God, and I expect a covenant people to make covenants and keep them." Psychology replies, "You may be a covenant God, but I'm not happy with the way things are going for me. I'm more concerned about how things are going than about doing things according to your principles, God."

We must get back to making sure that our psychology is governed by our theology, rather than allowing psychology to alter theology. God says, "Divorce do I hate because it is totally opposite to all that a covenant-making, covenant-keeping God stands for."

Here I am not suggesting that there are no circumstances in which divorce is permissible. I'm talking about flippant, casual divorce. What I am saying is that God declares *categorically*—he hates divorce. He has given it only as a concession because of the hardness of people's hearts, to protect people from the consequences of other people's hardness.

But we must be careful in the exercise of this freedom. The paramount concern is that our lives model what the covenant is, what faithfulness is.

If in our relationship with our spouse or with God there is any suggestion that covenant and faithfulness are being eroded, that should give us cause for concern. What does God call us to? He says, "Guard yourself in your spirit; do not break faith." Why? Because God does not break faith with us. That's who he really is. Our faithful God expects us to be faithful.

God's Justice

Next, the prophet says that God's justice is unchanged.

"You have wearied the Lord with your words," Malachi warns. " 'How have we wearied him?' you ask. By saying, 'All who do evil are good in the eyes of the Lord, and he is pleased with them' or 'Where is the God of justice?' " (2:17). The people have become skeptical about God's justice. They are saying: "God lets some people get away with murder, but others he watches with an eagle eye. He deals with some one way, and others another way. Where is the God of justice?"

We have now come to one of the greatest prophetic passages in the Bible. God says:

"See, I will send my messenger, who will prepare the way before me. Then suddenly the Lord you are seeking will come to his temple; the messenger of the covenant, whom you desire, will come," says the Lord Almighty.

But who can endure the day of his coming? Who can stand when he appears? For he will be like a refiner's fire or a launderer's soap. He will sit as a refiner and purifier of silver; he will purify the Levites and refine them like gold and silver. Then the Lord will have men who will bring offerings in righteousness, and the offerings of Judah and Jerusalem will be acceptable to the Lord, as in days gone by, as in former years. (3:1–4)

Here God is talking about the promise of a messenger. When this messenger comes people will not be able to tolerate the dramatic nature of his message. He will come like a refiner's fire. He will move through the priests—those who profess to serve the living God—and will purge from them all that is wrong. He will confront those who come near for judgment and will quickly testify against " '. . . sorcerers, adulterers and perjurers . . . who defraud laborers of their wages, who oppress the widows and the fatherless, and deprive aliens of justice, but do not fear me,' " (v. 5) says the just God.

What is God referring to here? The New Testament picks up on this passage and shows One who will come to the temple to purge the priesthood. Jesus himself will confront the priests with their sin in the name of a God of justice. None other than the Lord Jesus Christ himself will come. This passage has been applied by some to the cleansing of the temple by Jesus. God says to those who think that divine justice is a little wobbly at times: "Don't you worry about that, for finally and ultimately and eternally, justice will be done—and it will be done by the One whom God has appointed to be the judge, the One whom he will raise from the dead—even our Lord Jesus Christ." God's justice is unchanged, as well as his faithfulness, his glory, and his love.

God's Mercy

God's mercy is unchanged too: " 'I the Lord do not change. So you, O descendants of Jacob, are not destroyed. Ever since the time of your forefathers you have turned away from my decrees and have not kept them. Return to me, and I will return to you,' says the Lord Almighty. 'But you ask, "How are we to return?" Will a man rob God? Yet you rob me. But you ask, "How do we rob you?" In tithes and offerings' " (3:6–9).

Why weren't the descendants of Jacob destroyed? Because God does not change. He has been dealing with a very changeable, volatile group of people, the children of Israel. They are like Jacob their father, who was a real deceiver and conniver. He was always a handful for God to handle. And yet God was always merciful to him.

I often think of my mentor, Major Ian Thomas, from whom I learned so much about working with young people. He had a favorite expression as he looked at the young people who surrounded him at Capernwray: "Boys will be boys. But just be patient, and boys will be men."

That statement has given me a great deal of patience in my dealing with young people. God was patient with Jacob. He was saying, "Just be patient, and one of these days Jacob will get around to being Israel."

God looks down at us, I believe, and says, "Ordinary people will be ordinary people—but just be patient and one of these days they will get around to being what I want them to be." God's ongoing patient attitude encourages me.

In Malachi's time, things were becoming seriously wrong. People to whom God has been merciful and patient are now blatantly robbing him. And they won't even admit it. When Malachi in God's name confronts them with it, they simply ask, "How have we robbed you [God]?" Not one for backing off, Malachi replies, "In tithes and offerings."

Let me remind you of something. Rogue and rascal though he was, Jacob certainly paid his tithe. In the Old Testament, long before Moses, it was customary that a person pay his superiors one-tenth of his income. This had nothing to do with the Law of Moses. To say that the tithe is one-tenth is not to be totally accurate; it was far more than one-tenth. The tenth is a minimal amount. The Israelites were required by God to pay a kind of tax to the Levites which amounted to one-tenth of their income. This is how it worked: When they harvested their crops, one out of every ten sheaves was given to the Lord. When their flocks came out of the pasture, they would count the first one, the eleventh one, the twenty-first one, and so on. Whichever one came out as they counted was simply set off to one side. The tithe was straight off the top—one-tenth of all that was theirs was given to the Lord. Why should they tithe? They were making a statement concerning ownership and stewardship. The person handing over one-tenth of what he had was saying, "Someone else is truly the owner. I am not really the owner; I'm simply a steward of that which belongs to someone greater than I."

That is the key. In the principle of tithing, the person handing over one-tenth is saying, "You, God, are in reality the owner. In handing this over to you, I am admitting that I'm only a steward." Failing to give the tithe was failing to acknowledge the true owner.

This is what God is objecting to in Malachi. "I have been merciful to you," he says. "I own the land. I give you the crops. I give you all that you have. The only thing I ask from you in return is that you honor me, love me, and be faithful to me. I want you to demonstrate your appreciation of my mercy by giving me the tithe to show that I am the true owner and you are only the steward. But you have refused. You haven't done it. Therefore, you cannot expect my blessing upon your lives. If you're not openly admitting who the Lord is, you are not in a fit condition to experience my blessing."

What a word this is to the church today. While the New Testament doesn't speak of tithing as such, it does speak quite bluntly about proportionate giving out of a heart of gratitude. We should be saying two things to God: "All that is mine I have as a steward, because all that I have is truly yours." The person who does not give proportionately out of a joyful heart is a person who is denying that he is a steward. He is overlooking the fact that all we are and have belongs to the Lord. That is an insult to God's mercy.

I would like to see God's people so thrilled with his mercy, so excited about his ownership of everything and their stewardship of it, that they gladly give proportionately out of a full and thankful heart. God says, "If you return to me, I'll return to you." How do we return to him? One simple way is to put our hands into our pockets and give him what we should never have kept in the first place.

" 'Return to me,' " God says, " 'and I will return to you.' " This beautiful statement says bring the whole tithe, not a fraction, into the storehouse " 'that there may be food in my house. Test me in this,' says the Lord Almighty, 'and see if I will not throw open the floodgates of heaven and pour out so much blessing that you will not have room enough for it' " (3:10).

God's Purpose

One final thought: God's purpose is unchanged. At the end of Malachi's prophecy stands this marvelous statement concerning those who love the Lord: " '. . . the sun of righteousness will rise with healing in its wings' " (4:2).

It is clear who this "sun of righteousness" is—the Lord Jesus. What are the ultimate purposes of God? They are locked up in our Lord Jesus. He will appear in his great glory. This is an eschatological hope—something to look forward to as Christians. Those who are in God's will can expect to be preserved through his judgment. Those who are not in his will will suffer his fiery indignation. That is the ultimate purpose of God and he will be glorified. The last words of chapter 3 are very poignant at this point: " 'And you will again see the distinction between the righteous and the wicked, between those who serve God and those who do not.' "

As we come to the end of this book, we recall that the underlying theme has been to take God seriously. As we have looked at each of these minor prophets, we've endeavored to see something of the character and the nature of God revealed.

What have we seen in Malachi? That God is the One who does not change. We humans are the ones who change.

He is stable, solid. We're the ones who are unstable. He is the One who can be relied upon. We're the unreliable ones.

However, when we begin to take him seriously, we begin to get our lives in line with his. My wife Jill has a lovely expression. She used to think that prayer was sitting in a little dinghy pulling on the rope trying to get the big ship to come alongside. What she discovered was this. As she pulled the rope, her little dinghy was drawn alongside the big ship. Often our attitude is to try to get God (the big ship) alongside us. In actual fact what the Lord tells us to do is to pull on the rope and get ourselves alongside him. When we understand who he is, and what he is doing, then we have a chance to get our act together. But as long as we refuse to do that we will be in trouble.

A Summary

Remember these four final thoughts from Malachi: "Search your heart and honor me," says the Lord. Second, "Guard yourself in your spirit and don't break faith." Third, "Return to me and I will return to you." Finally, "Bring the whole tithe into the storehouse and prove me; see if I won't open the windows of heaven and pour out such a blessing that you will not be able to contain it," says the Lord. Think on this truth: "I the Lord change not."

This is the God with whom we have to do. He closes the Book of Malachi by telling us to wait patiently for the promise of his soon return. He is the one who closes the Old Testament itself by saying, "Take me seriously, and life will begin to make sense for you. I, the Lord, have promised it."